AF326514

THE STORIES Behind The Songs

DiElle

Printed in the United Kingdom
First Printing, 2020

ISBN: 978-1-8380231-0-2 (Paperback)
ISBN: 978-1-8380231-1-9 (eBook)

DiElle Music
Igloo Studios
Wickham, Hampshire
PO17 6JH

diellemusic.com

Discography

2009

Beautiful Monday

(See page 11)

2014

Fearless

(See page 51)

2017

Together

(See page 93)

2018

Strong

(See page 145)

2020

Candlelight

(See page 151)

Acknowledgements

There are so many people to thank that I fear if I begin to list people, I will unwittingly omit some. Suffice to say that I am grateful to everyone who's supported my journey in music, and me in the process of writing this book. I would like to show my gratitude to so many. Whatever I say will be inadequate, but here's trying.

Firstly, my family. My parents, Angela and Graham Cowles, were the first to show me the joy of music and have always been supportive, no matter how atypical my choices, and how many mistakes I make. I truly am blessed to have been born to them. My husband and stepdaughter, Chris and Caitlin Wood, for their support throughout this process, allowing me to share some of our personal journey.

My wider family and friends for their support through the tougher times, and sharing in the good times.

To my childhood friend Geoffrey Randell for being the one to show me that chasing my dreams was the only way to live. To his family and especially his sister Jayne for helping me write his story in this book. May this help his memory to live on, and the lessons I learned from him reach more people.

To every listener who took the time to tell me my music had touched you. Every artist needs that glimmer of encouragement, and it has spurred me on through the years, feeding my creativity. You let me know that my music could help people other than myself, which was a lesson I needed to learn. And the same goes for every radio show host, showcase producer, venue owner and blogger who showed an interest and made my music live further than me.

To everyone named in this book. You are part of this story and the tapestry of my life.

To every musician I have played with, recorded with and written with. You have all given me the greatest gift: to bring my songs to life. Especially Chris Wood and John Gleadall who have given me the most fulfilling band I have ever played in, with your humour, open mindedness, creativity, kindness, hard work, dedication, flexibility, willingness to sleep on freezing airport floors and go where the music has taken us.

The Stories Behind
The Songs...

Greetings, dear reader, and thank you for spending some of your precious time on this planet reading this book.

I hope that you will find these stories of interest and you will continue to live life to the full, follow your dreams, and love as much as you can.

I first started performing my own music in public when I was about 15 years old. Generally it was at open mic nights and jam nights where you would get to sing three songs or thereabouts. You'd sit amongst the audience before and after, and generally have the opportunity to interact with people who were interested in your music. This dialogue, that we would now call marketing, was socialised. It's funny that we've come full circle now and artists are seeking out a way to create dialogue with people who are moved by their art. I wish I'd known at the time what a gift it was to be able to speak to people in that way... This book is a tribute to them by answering, in the most complete way I could imagine, the question I was asked more than any other:

"What's the story behind that song then?"

This was before social media, before email, before you could digitally track everyone who came to your ticket page and be able to reach out to them at some point again in the future. I hope this book reaches some of those original people who put the idea in my head all those years ago, that people are actually moved by the context, creation and inspiration of art, not just the end result of it.

In the subsequent years, I have grown as an artist. In those early days I was fragile, unsure of myself, embarrassed and self-conscious doing anything other than singing. I'd deliberately sneak off and play where no one knew me ("I would only sing for strangers"), I didn't want to talk (I wrote songs because I didn't *want* to talk about it), I was an awkward, gawky, fat, unpopular kid with crooked teeth. At least, that's what I thought. I hated my body and hated people looking at me, I didn't know myself or my creative process, and I was not comfortable talking about what drives me to write. I didn't understand it myself. I actually felt affronted at the request for more background about my music, like they were being nosy, asking me such a personal question. At that time, I did not have the skills to satisfy the person asking the question without disclosing more than I was comfortable with. This is a skill I continue to hone and consider during my writing process now.

All I knew at the time was that I had an uncontrollable urge to create things. In fact I don't even know if that is true. I don't think I actually consciously knew that, I just did it. Music and art were the things that comforted me in my dark hours.

It is with the wisdom of hindsight that I now know that those people asking me questions, the radio interviews I took and audience members I chatted with, have been an integral part of my growth.

I feel it's important to tell you that this is not an autobiography. You will notice the passage of time and changes in circumstances that I have not explained, and that is because there was no song about those particular events. Whilst I put a huge amount of myself into everything I do, write from life experience and do share very personal circumstances that relate to the songs, it's important to tell you that this is all about the music.

However, these stories are just my experiences that gave rise to these songs, but I've learned that we all experience music differently; each listener has a truth about the music they listen to, which is equally valid. If you feel a song has another meaning and it resonates with a life experience of yours, who am I to argue?

Album: *Beautiful Monday*
Released: 31/03/2009 (Remastered 2014)

A special thank you

The *Beautiful Monday* album, released in March 2009, is a selected compilation of my acoustic work over the previous 10 years. We toured this album in 2009 across the UK and Republic of Ireland as an acoustic trio. Working in collaboration with Oxjam – a UK based music fundraising initiative launched by Oxfam in 2007 – we raised over £3000 for people living in poverty with *Beautiful Monday*. Thank you to everyone who made contributions.

The origins of Beautiful Monday...

Many of the songs on *Beautiful Monday* were written during the year I spent in Sri Lanka, 1999–2000. I was working with another English girl my age, Kate, in a rural part of the country, teaching conversational English to the local community and doing social work in a local children's hospital. Working in such close proximity to extreme poverty influenced me greatly at a young and impressionable age, and I was moved to write by way of making sense of what I was seeing around me.

The children valued their education greatly, and everywhere we went people treated us like princesses. Children were dying in the hospital from completely preventable diseases, simply from lack of resources. Dirty water and lack of education about basic hygiene were spreading diseases like malaria and HIV. It was a complete shock to the system, and being my first time away from home, I needed some therapeutic means of coming to terms with this harsh reality. Many of the songs on the *Beautiful Monday* album were inspired directly or indirectly by our experiences, and the mettle I had to find inside myself to work in that environment for a whole year.

Basic values such as love, kindness and friendship are common themes throughout this album. When life is stripped so bare of material things, people's values become so much more visible. So often it was the people who had nothing at all who would offer the clothes on their back with a smile on their face. I felt these experiences guided me towards what I really wanted out of life, and taught me to be true to myself. I haven't always managed that in the intervening years, but feel that my time in Sri Lanka was a cornerstone in my life where I was following my heart and doing what I truly believed to be the best, most valuable use of my time on this earth. For that I will be forever grateful. It has truly been a privilege to sell my music to raise funds for communities in extreme poverty like the ones we were working with in Sri Lanka, to give back to them where I feel I gained so much. I hope you enjoy these stories.

When we started planning the Beautiful Monday tour, we had a goal for how much money we were aiming to raise. I had heard about an Oxfam fundraising campaign to help people across Africa. We wanted to raise enough money for water and food storage facilities for two villages. This would enable two villages to store clean water, avoiding waterborne diseases like malaria, which are the main killers of young children. The amount raised also paid for grain storage, enabling people to keep their crops throughout the year, avoiding famine. This amounted to £1200 – not an insubstantial goal, we thought. Over the 12 dates of the Beautiful Monday tour, this meant we had to raise £100 at each gig.

Given that we were travelling out of our home area, playing original music that local people would not know, we knew we had our work cut out for us. I was nervous. The Oxjam promotions team were able to give us a little bit of local help, but as it was all run on volunteer power, naturally some members had less time and fewer resources to help us than others. It came to the tour launch on 31st March 2009, and we pulled out all the stops to raise what we could and be sent off with a splash. A brewery donated a barrel of Fosters which was a fantastic opportunity to have posters emblazoned with 'Drink Fosters to End Poverty' plastered all over our home town. On the day, our real-ale-loving music fans dutifully drank the Fosters without too much complaint... Although they did point it out... but they weren't complaining.

An amazing £500 was raised at that gig through album sales and donations – a fantastic way to send us off. We set off on our merry way, thrilled to be ahead of schedule with the fundraising before we'd left home.

Some gigs on the tour were great, and very supportive, some less so, but we trotted on. Before the end of the tour we had more than surpassed our original target, and were on the way to raising enough for the seventh village.

We will forever be grateful to everyone who supported the Beautiful Monday tour, not only by donating money, but by giving time, publicity and support. So many people helped us, which enabled us to raise this amazing total of money – far more than we could ever have dreamed of. Six whole villages of men, women and children living without food and clean water – that's an amazing difference to have made to the lives of so many people. Thank you.

Beautiful Monday album artwork

The original limited edition print of this album featured a hand-drawn sunflower on a blue background donated by an artist for the cause. When it came to remastering *Beautiful Monday* in time for the *Fearless* launch in 2014, the artwork was updated. Originally the songs for *Beautiful Monday* were pretty much all recorded in one day, as this was intended to be a side project of my band at the time. We were recording our rock pop album *Strangers* and this was a distraction. Consequently it was all a bit raw and very rushed. The intention with remastering it was to rectify a lot of these issues, but when it came to it, in true *Beautiful Monday* style, it was right down to the wire, and we remastered the whole thing overnight, driving the master disc to Cheltenham at 4am in order to get them printed in time.

The only musician still with me from the original project was my bass player Greg. He was just starting to make his way into music full time and had found himself covering a science lesson in a school he was teaching in. He took this photograph of a sunflower seed, and I asked him if I could use it for the new artwork. I loved the sunflower connection, and the feeling that the seed was feeding into the ideas of new beginnings. Greg took the seed home and germinated it, and when it got too big for his flat he brought it round to mine, so we shared looking after it.

Beautiful Monday has taken on its own identity as, at the time of writing, I am doing a weekly broadcast interviewing interesting people and bringing positivity at the beginning of the week. Named after the album and song, sunflowers have become a symbol of the broadcast too. I have been so amazed at how this has reached people who need a little bit of a lift at the beginning of the week, that this may also become a book at some point.

Track 1:
Beautiful Monday

Some people say the week's too long
The weekend sunshine always gone
I know it rained on Friday
Was cold the whole night through
But there's a brand new light babe
And it's shining for you
It's a Beautiful Monday

Beautiful Monday

Some people say don't hope too hard
Tie up your pipedreams in the yard
Don't try and it can't hurt you
You're safe the whole night through
But there's a brand new fight babe
And it's spoiling for you
It's a Beautiful Monday

Beautiful Monday

It's a beautiful day
Beautiful Monday.

'Beautiful Monday' is both a figurative and literal song, inspired by the day my work was first published by Acorn Music Group in 2008. 'Lou's Song', my first single, had been released with B-side 'Twinkle', two very personal songs of mine, on Monday 28th April 2008. Having not had a great experience of music at school I had always believed that I was never going to be good enough – as a singer, a songwriter or musician – and that I had a snowball's chance in hell of being recorded or professionally published. In fact my only goal for years was to have my own digital 8track at home so I could get down all my ideas.

'Beautiful Monday' was inspired by the release of 'Lou's Song', with me having felt that I had turned a new corner and the possibilities were now endless. The record industry was undergoing much change, and the canvas seemed blank.

Figuratively, 'Beautiful Monday' is my way of rebelling against all the people who, directly or indirectly, have belittled my ambitions over the years – I have come to realise that the only person who can stand in the way of pursuing your dreams is you. I learned the worst thing you can do is to not even try, and live a half life wondering what could have been if you had only had the courage to try.

People had given me advice about 'being realistic', and advised me to have a 'back-up plan' and a 'proper job'. The years I tried that made me miserable beyond expression. I couldn't live for Friday nights, chained to a desk job I hated, crippled by fear from living the life I wanted. It takes all sorts to make the world go round, but beyond exams and bills and other life administration, you have to be true to what makes you happy.

Never lose sight of your dreams.

Track 2:
I Won't Get In Your Way

I know it was all my fault
I should have known what to say
But I won't do it next time
I won't get in your way
No I won't get in your way
Again

It happened again
But it's not what it seems
You're still the man I fell for
You're still the man of my dreams
I just won't get in your way
Again

I'll just ignore the bruises you've left inside and out
Sweep up the broken glass, I won't scream and shout
I won't try to run away coz I know we'll work it out
I won't cry out loud, that's not what love's about
No I won't get in your way again

I know you didn't mean it
You would never raise your hand
It was just the drink that was talking
You work hard, I understand
And I won't get in your way
Again

I'll just ignore the bruises you've left inside and out
Sweep up the broken glass, I won't scream and shout
I won't try to run away coz I know we'll work it out
I won't cry out loud, that's not what love's about
No I won't get in your way again

But I couldn't leave now if I wanted to
Coz you've taken all I had
My friends, my home, my heart, my soul,
Made me see I'm bad
Even if I wanted to I've got nowhere to go
But it doesn't matter now
Coz we'll work it out, I know

I'll just ignore the bruises you've left inside and out
Sweep up the broken glass, I won't scream and shout
I won't try to run away coz I know we'll work it out
I won't cry out loud, that's not what love's about
No I won't get in your way again

I know you mean it this time
Though you've promised me before
Every day you don't have fists for me
I love you a little more
And I won't get in your way
I won't get in your way
No I won't get in your way
No I won't get in your way
Again

'I Won't Get In Your Way', I am grateful to say, was not derived from direct life experience. We learned a great deal about the way some Sri Lankans traditionally approach marriage and relationships. We knew many people whose marriages had been arranged, we knew couples where the men were happily having affairs as a matter of course, the women seemingly passive and downtrodden, and we knew that some men were violent towards their wives. To two young, independent western women, these ideas seemed abhorrent, primitive, and something that we would never be at risk of experiencing.

Incidentally, as we grew to understand the society more, we learned that arranged marriages actually worked very well for those who believed in them, and many people were very happy. Arranged marriage did not necessarily equal an abusive relationship, or an unhappy coupling. Enlightenment begins.

However, when I returned to the UK, I was shocked to discover that someone I used to work with was in a destructive and violent relationship. She was an intelligent, educated, assertive woman and I couldn't understand how this man had gotten under her skin so much that she wouldn't just leave him. It was so clear he was never going to change for the better. She would make excuses for him and look for any reason to stay and be hopeful; her self-esteem had been completely eroded and it was like she had undergone a strange kind of institutionalisation within the relationship. Completely controlled by it, yet dependent on its walls also. It was so painfully sad to watch. But as I found out more about domestic violence I realised how much of it there is around, and how frightening the statistics are. It's not just an issue in underdeveloped countries. It knows no boundaries of race, social status or means. I tried to put myself in her shoes to understand more about what she was going through, and 'I Won't Get In Your Way' was the result.

I did come to realise that I had to explain at least in part when we played this live, because people did just assume I was speaking from personal experience. An important lesson in performance art, and assumptions made about singer-songwriters. That experience informed my songwriting craft, and I would go on to consider how I presented things from a songwriting level. If things were a bit too raw, I would find a way of softening it to make it more palatable in a live context; that way I could keep people with me more, rather than just shocking them. If they're with you, you might have the chance to tell a story, to educate, to win sympathy for something thus far unconsidered. It all went in the melting pot.

Track 3:
Sapphire Tears

I know you're hurting
And I know you don't want to say it out loud
But you don't have to be the tower of strength
You don't have to be so proud

When you're shattered like lead crystal
Into a thousand pieces, know
That I'd hold them in my hand
And I won't let go

Let me be there
When you're backed up to the wall
Let me be there
When you're trying to make sense of it all
Let me be there
To cry sapphire tears for you
You don't have to do it all alone
You're never on your own

We've run a long road together
From the playground when we were six years old
We've shared our stormy weather
You've been my log fire in the freezing cold

When the cruel labyrinth tangles
Into a thousand tunnels, know
That I'll pace right beside you
And I won't let go

Let me be there
When you're backed up to the wall
Let me be there
When you're trying to make sense of it all
Let me be there
To cry sapphire tears for you
You don't have to do it all alone
You're never on your own

Let me be there
When the rain starts to fall
Let me be there
When you're trying to make sense of it all
Let me be there to cry sapphire tears for you
You don't have to do it all alone
You're never on your own
You're never on your own

As you will read later on in this book, I spent a lot of my time in Sri Lanka healing from a very difficult year. The year previously I had lost a friend, Geoff, in a car accident – my first experience of losing someone of my generation. This tragedy had been incredibly difficult to accept, and totally traumatic for his family. I had known him since I was two years old, and it remains to this day one of the most difficult experiences I have had to come to terms with in my life. Especially learning to live with the remaining love in my heart for someone I would never see again, and that I never said goodbye to him when there was the slightest chance that he could have heard me.

Also that year I had my heart broken for the first time, and we had lost my nanna, a close family member, so all in all it was a year of bereavement for me and many people very close to me. Throughout this difficult time, I was very lucky to have some very special people around me, helping me to pick up the pieces. These are the people who make life bearable when life throws awful things at us, and I will always be grateful for their love and support.

'Sapphire Tears' was inspired by the desire of wanting to return the favour, and hoping that these people would trust me and come to me when they were going through tough times. Trusting someone enough to allow yourself to be vulnerable with them can be extremely difficult. It's an honour and a privilege to be trusted, as well as to trust, in my view. 'Sapphire Tears' is the emotion of reassuring people they don't need to be proud or brave, and they don't have to suffer alone, as we would go to the ends of the earth for them, incorporating our own need to comfort them.

Track 4:
Mahogany Radio

We used to listen to vinyl on the mahogany radio
He'd talk and I would listen about the things that I should know
Once he told me a story about a picture of the queen
And that mahogany radio was a comfort in my teens

I took that comfort with me as twice I packed my bags
Spent time in places with lions and dragons on their flags
And when it seemed that homewards was the last way I would go
I had the music inside me from the mahogany radio

At times the world has been tuneless, blowing the gale of the fight
Now I'm tuned in to radio hopeful, and I know it will be alright

The years skip by into adulthood and the winds become less wild
Thrice I returned to the lion, and each time felt like a child
But at home with the vinyl playing, no end to what he would give
Those nights with mahogany radio taught me how to live
That mahogany radio taught me how to live

'Mahogany Radio' is actually a story about the musical education given to me by my dad. We used to listen to his old records on a record player and radio in a mahogany cabinet in our lounge. Through the years when I was growing up we would listen to albums that were important to him in his youth, and he would tell me stories and we'd talk and put the world to rights. Once, he told me a story about a picture of the queen.

Dad was a photographer in London as a younger man, and was busy with weddings, models and events. At one of these special events, a royal flotilla on the Thames, he was devastated to discover he had the flash on the wrong setting, having taken a few precious snaps of our gracious queen. Of course, he was in purgatory until he could develop the photos (no digital picture on the back of the screen in those days, and just a few precious frames per roll of film), and he had to wait several excruciating hours to discover it was actually fine. He never forgot this.

I developed a taste in my formative years for Carole King, Lennon and McCartney, Bob Dylan, Joni Mitchell, The Eagles, The Hollies, The Stones, Lindisfarne, Simon and Garfunkel and many more great songwriters who expressed life experience and human emotion through exquisitely crafted songs. I spent many hours listening to these records lying on the carpet with my head between the speakers, and whenever I felt unsure during the turbulent years of my adolescence, I always found comfort somewhere in that record collection.

When I left home for the first time and moved to Sri Lanka, a place with a lion on its flag, I literally 'took that comfort' with me, having taped as much as I could, and my mum sent more out to me later. I spent many years globetrotting and trying to find where I fit in the world, but I always had that music to comfort me and remind me where my heart lived, and how I wanted to live my life.

That mahogany radio taught me how to live.

Track 5:
Shelter From The Storm
For Isobelle

The first time your mother heard you laughing
The first time your daddy saw you cry
Open up your eyes and see the sunshine
We dreamed of all the things you'd ever try

And we'll do our best to shelter you from every storm
Wrap you up and keep you safe and warm
Show you all the love and strength and courage
That arrived the day that you were born

Each time a cloud becomes a castle
Each time you learn something new
Every time your soul is touched with wonder
Our hearts and souls will be touched too

And we'll do our best to shelter you from every storm
Wrap you up and keep you safe and warm
Show you all the love and strength and courage
That arrived the day that you were born

And on those days when the sun won't shine
We'll be on our way, put your hand in mine

And we'll do our best to shelter you from every storm
Wrap you up and keep you safe and warm
Show you all the love and strength and courage
That arrived the day that you were born

'Shelter From The Storm', quite simply, was written for my goddaughter. Isobelle is the firstborn of my very special friend Kate who spent that year with me in Sri Lanka. We became exceptionally close, and I was touched to be asked to be godparent to Isobelle. So when the time came for the christening, Kate asked me if I would sing something at the service – she didn't mind what, she just wanted me to sing. Of course I agreed.

I had started to look for something and couldn't find the right song that reflected what I wanted to say exactly, so naturally I began to write something. Artistically at the time, I was in the midst of a commercial period of writing, overly concerned with hooks and being radio friendly. When I sat down to write Isobelle's song, commercial viability couldn't have been further from my mind; I couldn't care less if it was radio friendly, and just wrote from my heart to hers. 'Shelter From The Storm' was the result. The first incarnation of this song was a simple arrangement, with completely acoustic vocals and piano. Just raw and real.

This is one of those songs that came out almost seamlessly from start to finish, as if I was the medium of the muse. It doesn't always happen like that for me but I love it when it does. Sometimes I feel like the song is just coming through me, like it's 'none of my business'. When the ideas are clear, the song often takes shape quickly for me, like a bud becoming a bloom.

It was a complete honour to be asked to have such a special role in Isobelle's life, and in its first instance this song was intended to be akin to a lullaby that I imagined would be crooned to her gently as a small baby. Possibly night after night as she perhaps wasn't sleeping.

Being a bit of a softie, I just about managed to perform it at her christening without crying, despite mascara running all over the house! I just sang it directly to Isobelle who was sitting contentedly in Kate's lap. Kate told me afterwards that she used every ounce of self-control not to cry as she knew that it would start me off if she did, but that she'd found it so hard because I was singing forthrightly in her direction!

It seems to resonate with parents and godparents in cultures all around the globe. I wrote that song with nothing but Isobelle in mind, however I'm so happy it's touched so many people. It is wonderful that since then Isobelle's song has been played and performed at christenings and baby naming ceremonies in every continent.

Track 6:
The Heron

The heron stood and he looked at me
Began to fly away
Then he said 'come follow me'
So I spread my wings
And flew from the nest
In my tree

Fly, fly
Wait for me
In the sky

So we flew over the lake
At Kandalama
And I saw my life anew
And the heron he saw me smile
Told me 'you can fly
You don't need my wings
You just need you, and yours'

So fly,
Fly
Don't wait for me
I'll meet you in the sky

So when my heron
Flies through my mind
I have to know that I am brave I'll make it home
And the feeling that I'm alone
Flies away

'The Heron' is a story about leaving home, flying the nest, for the first time. This was written in Sri Lanka inspired by a real heron I saw by the lake in our first few days in Kandalama, the remote location where we were to be based for the duration of our placement. Our project was hosted by an incredible hotel named after the location. Designed by Geoffrey Bawa, the hotel was built into the side of the mountain, embracing the rocks and wrapped in jungle. However, we did not live in the stunningly gorgeous hotel. We lived in the humble staff village along the road, sharing a room, 15 feet square. It was a culture shock. We were homesick. We barely knew each other. The enormity of what we'd undertaken was sinking in. I wasn't sure I'd made the right decision. I wasn't sure I was able to feel excited about it yet.

We had arrived a couple of days previously after a two-day journey, and emotional roller coaster of leaving all our family and friends for a whole year at the tender age of 18. We were exploring our immediate surroundings, and close to our living quarters was a large reservoir, or 'tank', as they were called locally. The first weekend, we were walking along the waterline of the tank, coming to terms with the absence of nightclubs, when we saw a large white heron at the water's edge. It was one of the most beautifully exotic things I had ever seen in my life, and I felt the rush of new experience. As we walked closer the heron spread its enormous wings and took flight.

That heron became a metaphor for growing into the person I needed, to be able to do the work we were doing in the local community, and adjust to life in the jungle. I see that experience, that beautiful wingspan, in my mind's eye every time we perform that song.

Track 7:
Strangers

All the time I wished away made me say
I would only sing for strangers
All the tears I wiped away, everyday made me say
That I'd only sing for strangers

I know why you hate me
Why you look at me and ask who
It's coz you hate yourself
And you think I'm a reflection of you
Reflection of you

All the time I wished away made me say
I would only sing for strangers
Even though I'm far away you will stay close to me
Coz we're not strangers

I know why you forgot me
Why you think of me and ask who
It's coz you forget yourself
And you think I'm a reflection of you
Reflection of you

All the things we left unsaid
All the things floating in our heads
You would have known what to do with me
You would have known if you could see
This is the inside of me

You never saw me inside coz you were blind
And now we're strangers
You never saw me inside

I started writing 'Strangers' when I was about 17 and only had about half of it. The other half came to me the first night I was in my bed in the room at Kandalama that would be my home for the coming year. I gigged this song as a solo artist for a long time, then when we started rehearsing it with the band it changed shape again, and rearranged itself yet again for going back to acoustic work.

As it was written so disjointedly when I was so young, I don't think I ever consciously knew what it was really 'about' until we started recording it. Many of the lyrics were inspired by different people in my life, some who had stayed, some who had come and gone, and some who had caused heartache. I met so many people in my time in Sri Lanka who became very close to me, some of whom we could hardly communicate with, because of the language barrier.

Somehow we managed with various hand gestures, and card games – '2s and 10s' became a regular feature of our social life, quite a contrast from the pubs and clubs in the UK. Some people who had come into our lives seemed to teach everlasting lessons by doing very little, such as an eight-month-old girl with cerebral palsy from a poverty stricken family, whose big brown eyes and simple joyous smile I will never forget. I think 'Strangers' is about the changing nature of relationships, the confusion that can ensue, how surprisingly difficult it can be to communicate with people.

I think we can all have a tendency to fill in the gaps ourselves, and try to 'mind read' what we assume people are thinking or feeling, and I certainly felt that I was never good at communicating my real feelings when I was growing up. I don't think I was very good at even understanding them myself, and believe that this continues to be incredibly hard for a lot of people deep into adulthood.

Communication is so integral to all relationships that it can make people who are close in some ways strangers in others. Similarly, sometimes I think people find it easier to be truthful with people we don't know at all, so sharing with a stranger an intimate connection. Have you ever had that experience of sitting next to a stranger on the bus and getting their life story before your journey ends?

'Strangers' is one of those songs that came together with the band quickly and became a powerful song for us, making itself the title track of the full rock band album. However, I still gig it acoustically as a solo artist and it is always well received, despite its lack of transparency lyrically.

Perhaps it's ambiguous enough that people find some truth about themselves in it. The listeners make their own truth of all songs anyway; at least I hope they do.

Track 8:
The Windmill

In her hair she wore a crown of cornflowers,
And the windmill was her home
She had been kissed, but only by a thistle
And been loved by a stone
She dreamed of black water on silver shores
She'd walk with her lover, someone she'd adore
But after half a million tick tocks more, coz
No one can make time stand still

At the inn his ale tasted dirty
And his knife and fork were cold
He wonders what's the point of being happy
With a soul that's tired and old
He dusted the rust from her wedding ring
No day in the church, no anthem to sing
He spent half a million hours aching, but
No one can make time stand still

When sunset came he strolled up to the windmill
And he saw her in the light
Instantly his heart forgot its torment
And as the day became the night
He stepped forward and reached out his arm
To see just a corn dolly rest in his palm
If life is the storm maybe love is the calm
No one can make time stand still

In Clanfield, near Queen Elizabeth Country Park, in deepest green England, on top of a hill, there is a beautiful old windmill. Windmills have always appeared to have some kind of magical, mystical quality to me since childhood. Perhaps it was the idea of capturing something as elusive as the wind, and using it to make something as real as flour. It happens that this particular windmill is visible from the seat of a rather beautiful piano, where I was moved to write.

On the surface, 'The Windmill' is a rather surreal winter love story, about a fictitious, broken-hearted man who fell in love with a corn dolly.

Underneath, 'The Windmill' explores the human tendency to see something or believe something that isn't really there; to find that what you think is true is not, to live through seemingly endless pain, and still find love to give; that when all around us is confusing and tempestuous, the human ability to love can be calming, while at other times, love itself is the storm.

But 'no one can make time stand still'; no matter what we live through and manage to bear, nobody can stop time. The more we try to live, the faster the years rush by us, and the more we hurt, the more time we want to heal.

Time is the one thing we all share – whether business tycoon, royalty or homeless on the street, we all have the same amount of time, regardless of power, status or influence.

It can't be stopped, it can't be controlled and we can't make more of it.

The only choice we have is over what we do with the time we have, heartbroken or not. And that is something that motivates me every single day.

Track 9:
The End Of The Road

So here we stand at the end of the road
There's no light and it's cold
But you know that I
Have to say goodbye
But I'll remember our time
For the rest of my life

So you go your way and I'll go mine
There's no hope and no time
But the day that I
Knew I had to cry
You said 'things have changed, and so have I'
Well I guess things have changed,
And so have I
Now everything's changed forever
And so have I

'The End Of The Road' is a simple story about the first time my heart was broken. It is actually the final piece of a five song project I had been writing since I was 18, about the stages of falling in love: meeting someone; falling for them and being together; the moment you realise it is not working out; breaking up; and then moving on and letting go.

Unfortunately the fourth song in this project was missing for many years, and I still had not written it by the time the original *Stories Behind The Songs* eBook for *Beautiful Monday* was being written. This elusive fourth song appeared on *Fearless*, completely out of context, over 10 years after I started this project of the heartbreak epic. But by that time, the original story had been lost. 'The End Of The Road' is the last of the five songs, representing the time you know you have to move on and let go.

I spent much time in Sri Lanka healing from this first experience of heartbreak, and felt that 'The End Of The Road' was the expression of what should be a 'crossroads', but not wanting to take either road.

Too hurt to look back and reluctant to move forwards, the end of the road.

<h1 style="text-align:center">Track 10:
Lou's Song</h1>

A real friend is someone who's always there
Someone who doesn't need to tell you that they care
Someone to hug when you're feeling blue
Someone special, someone like you

A real friend is someone who shares your pain
Someone who stands beside you in the sunshine and the rain
To be your anchor when you're lost at sea
Someone to depend on, someone like thee

Someone who walks you through the good times
Shares your troubles, toasts your wine
To hold you up after that 15th vodka shot
To cry a little, laugh a lot

A real friend will be there whether far or near
A hand to hold, someone to hear
And you know that there's just no need to say
That that's the way it is and it'll always be that way

And when the hard times they come your way
And you feel you're nearing the end of the day
Stand together side by side and see it through
With someone you trust, someone like you

'Lou's Song' was written during my time in Sri Lanka, and the first of my songs to be professionally published in 2007. It was inspired by the real-life experience of having a wonderfully loyal and steady best friend from the age of six.

When I went to Sri Lanka, this was the longest time we had not seen each other, yet her friendship made me strong even from this great distance.

Whilst inspired by one true experience of friendship, 'Lou's Song' is also a testament to the horrible life experiences we can endure when we have good friends around us. My friend Kate, who became extremely close to me in our time together in Sri Lanka, has become a bedrock of my life, and a haven I retreat to when I need respite.

Kate and I shared a very small room during the time we were away together, and she was witness to my writing process for many of these songs, but particularly this one. I distinctly remember her telling me the first draft of this song was 'bohomo lasanai' (very beautiful), and so I was moved to make it a first choice for recording when we returned.

It was the first of my songs to be published, and a true testament to where I stand in life and as an artist. My most fundamental value.

Bonus Track 1:
Twinkle

The laughter in your smile
The twinkle in your eye
Your outlook was always bright
And you could never tell a lie
So thank you for all our time
And all of your advice
You told things how they were
And how to put it right

And so to learn from you
Half full is the glass
Don't focus on life's wrongs
And don't dwell on the past

The sunshine in your smile
The twinkle in your eye
Your outlook was always bright
And you could never tell a lie
A new day begins every morning
And for every bad day there's a good one
Waiting around the corner

'Twinkle' was not actually included on the original edition of the *Beautiful Monday* album, but was released as the B-side to 'Lou's Song' in 2007. I wrote 'Twinkle' for my grandfather who died very suddenly in 2006. I wrote and recorded this in the days between his death and his funeral, and it was played at his funeral service.

Although it had been a terrible shock to all of my family to lose Gramps so suddenly, he was an optimistic and frank man, and I wanted to remember his essence and spirit in a positive way.

He now rests under an oak in the English countryside, befitting to the role he had in our family. I have never performed this live, however it has been wonderful to hear from music fans that this song has been a comfort to others when they have lost loved ones.

When this album was remastered in 2014 this track was included on the listing.

Bonus Track 2:
Mister Merchandise

Mr. Merchandise is on every street, if you got
Somethin' to trade then he'll be there to greet
Even if you haven't he'll give it all he's got
And you'll end up buying something if you like it or not

Mr Merchandise he does it so well
Mr Merchandise and his hard sell
He'd get you to buy a snowball
If you were en route to hell
Mr. Merchandise

Mr. Merchandise can get you a watch
Talk you into purchasing a kick in the crotch
He'll tell you there's a refund, money back guarantee
But instead you go to China with a sack of his tea

He sells the snow to Eskimos, he sells tartan paint
Once he even sold goodwill to a saint
You wanna trade your soul, he'll quote you a price
He's Mr. Merchandise

This picture is of me backstage with two beautiful souls in my life, Chris Wood (right) and John Gleadall (left). Both are fabulous musicians that I have the pleasure to play with from time to time, and some days I have to pinch myself, realising just how lucky I am to get to make music with people like this. This is just before the Acoustic Club gig in March 2017.

Backstage selfie at the Ashcroft Arts Centre

I always loved arts centres and dreamed of the days I'd be able to perform in them. The dressing room at the Ashcroft is wonderful because it has all the posters of all the fantastic artists who have performed there. I was at some of those gigs and they made a huge impression on me as a young musician.

We performed this track from the *Beautiful Monday* album at this gig, and I remembered during the soundcheck that I was actually inspired to write it in the very room we were performing in. I had been to see Jane Taylor perform and had been inspired by her jazzy approach to folk music. Just before the end of the show, she mentioned that she'd be outside by her merchandise stall if anyone wanted CDs signing and so on. Those two things collided in my head and I came up with 'Mister Merchandise' – a story about a shady man who would sell you anything just to make a buck... (no reflection on Jane!).

The funny thing is, my dad has said more than once that he thought this song was about him! He has been an entrepreneur since the tender age of 15, and built his own business up from nothing. He has been involved with many trades, settling on horticulture when I was about five years old. Before settling on horticulture, he was involved in buying and selling property, and used to tell stories about sending a young guy to the shop to get tartan paint, which is where that came from, so I guess his influence is in there somewhere. (Dad also taught me how to spell 'mister' when I was tiny and thought Mr. was the spelling.)

Dad does love a good wind-up, but I never saw him as this shady, sell-you-anything rip-off merchant — because he isn't! That picture was a culmination of shady characters I met while travelling, always trying to rip off unsuspecting tourists, and probably too much time watching *Only Fools and Horses* as a youngster.

On the record this is double bass and vocals only, originally intended to be included on the *Fearless* album. However due to artistic differences with the producer of *Fearless*, 'Mister Merchandise' didn't make it onto that album; we included it as a bonus track of the 2014 remaster of *Beautiful Monday*, where it probably does sit better in terms of tone. Greg and I always played it live like that, bass or double bass and vocals, similar to the style Peggy Lee sings 'Fever', but I am also very much enjoying playing this fuller live version with John and Chris.

Album: *Fearless*
Released: 27/04/2014

To write this book and not discuss the controversy over this image would, I think, be a missed opportunity to contextualise my artistic choices. The image on all of my albums is intended to describe more about what you can expect from the music. *Beautiful Monday* was simple, *Together* was technicoloured, and *Fearless* was bare. This image is a photoshopped version of a charcoal drawing (by Kate Simms) of a photograph of me (taken by Beth Whitley). So it is me, although that's not what was particularly important. The message is the representation of facing vulnerability. I realise there are people who can't see past the nudity; they don't see the imagery or the metaphor, and I knew that would be a risk. But I had to take it. As with the rest of this album, I was not willing to compromise, as I will relate.

This image describes the music in its emotionally raw state, and is a symbol of me shedding the disappointments and the unmet expectations of previous projects and life choices that had left me artistically unfulfilled, sometimes heartbroken. It could have been anyone in the picture, as the 'baring all' was a metaphor, but I guess the fact that it was me just deepened my reasoning. Also, having had body image issues since I was a small child, it was an exercise in learning to accept myself the way I am, another huge step at such a turbulent time in my life, and one that has liberated me in many other ways. I was going through a nasty separation at the time, after a toxic and dysfunctional relationship that threatened to leave me feeling like a failure on every level, not least as a woman and an artist. *Fearless* embodies more of those struggles than I realised at the time.

I loved *Beautiful Monday*; it wakened me. I loved *Strangers* – the 10-track rock-pop album that had major label interest, that was 90% done and never released. It excited me, but I knew it wasn't really 'me'. But *Fearless*...

Fearless set me free.

Fearless was the album that opened doors I didn't even know were there... and I got validation as an artist from someone I had not really realised I was trying desperately to impress. Me.

I finally felt like this was the album that represented me as a creative. I didn't care if it was commercially viable; I didn't care if any of it got radio play. I had the songs on it I wanted; they were recorded, arranged and produced how I wanted them and I took great pains to make that so. I had the musicians I wanted play on it, and with the joy of technological advances, it didn't matter where they were geographically. We had real strings – something an earlier producer had told me was never worth the cost. I couldn't disagree more. Listen to the strings on the title track and tell me that wasn't worth it.

It was three years in the making during an exceptionally turbulent time in my life; a Herculean effort creatively, practically and financially. During a time when it would definitely have been easier to give up, it took a huge amount of courage on my part to see this through and retain the bare honesty in the music that I so desperately desired at that point. That gave rise to the title track, but also the artwork.

Knowing in my heart that that was the image I wanted, I had several discussions with a variety of people to see what their thoughts on it would be.

Almost everyone thought it was a bad idea.

All that did was strengthen my resolve.

It made me realise how much the image embodied my feelings at the time, although it took me a while to articulate that. A close friend from university, Naomi (a song on *Together* is inspired by her), said that she felt the image took the edge off the word 'fearless' which could have been interpreted as a word of warmongering violence. By showing soft, feminine vulnerability in the image it took on more of a representation of the music.

I had several meetings with Kate Simms, the artist, who seemed completely at ease with what I was asking. As an experienced life-drawing artist, she completely understood what I was looking for. I think that's why I liked the charcoal one the best too. Bare, no frills, all completely natural, no apologies. It is what it is, take it or leave it.

There have been some people who have not been able to see past the image long enough to consider that viewpoint, some who have considered it offensive, and some who considered it controversial, but still I have no regrets. Perhaps those people would have listened to and enjoyed the music if the image had been different, but at what artistic sacrifice to myself? *Fearless* had to be the album that was my legacy at that time, and without that artwork it would have been incomplete. The fulfilment I experienced of it being exactly what I wanted at all costs was an incredible lesson. This has not always been the case since – I have been happy to give and take on subsequent works – but trusting my instinct to know that at that point in my life, I was just not willing to compromise, to hell with the consequences, was actually a wonderful life lesson for me. Learning to hear my instincts, and trust them, was liberating and incredibly powerful. I apologise if the image offends you, inasmuch as I am sorry you feel offended, but I do not apologise for creating my work as I wanted it. Once it was complete, I knew I was standing on the ground I'd been trying to get to all my life. For that, I cannot be sorry. As you will learn in this book, it led to opportunities I could not have dreamed of.

Track 1:
No One To Thank Or Blame

Turn your face to the rain, and onward
Steel yourself for the game, and onward
You stand alone, no one to thank
You stand alone, no one to blame

This song became known by my old bandmates as 'Arty-Farty'. In my rebellion against commercial viability, I just indulged in the sound-scape style of song, ignoring everything I know about hook writing, song structure and radio friendly formats. The day I wrote this I was angry about the horrible situation I found myself in, disappointed and let down, yet determined it was not going to get me down. I would fight on, even if I had to do it alone, and then I would only have myself to blame, rather than being angry that someone had let me down or lied to me.

It started as a vocal and piano idea, and I explored the moody space of this simple, short piece. Slowly we added instruments and built up a cinematic canvas that reflected how I felt. I enjoyed balancing the track, keeping the softly sung vocals forward in the mix and the louder sung parts further back, toying with the idea of creating space and distance, adding the sound effects of birdsong in a thunderstorm, which was another symbol of how I felt in a way. A small but clear voice in a storm. At the time, I didn't think this would ever get any attention, any radio play or any fans; it was the quintessential, artistically indulgent 'album track' that I made just for the artistic fulfilment of painting my emotions with sound.

As it turns out, this piece opened doors for me I didn't know were there. By the wonder that is modern social media, I was introduced to an independent film producer who was looking for something 'moody with strings and female vocal' for the closing scene of a film she was producing. I sent her a link to this song and she loved it, immediately asking if I would be open to them using it for the closing titles of the film. Thinking about it for approximately three seconds, I said yes of course, and we got talking. She told me more about her current projects and let me know that she was hoping to have one artist compose the whole score for this film, and tentatively asked me if I'd be interested in doing it. Again, without knowing how or when at this point, I said yes, of course, and just thought – I'll figure this out later! This film is a psychological thriller called *The Girl In A Coma*, and at the time of writing is still in development. Whether or not this film ever gets made, it opened my eyes to the world of film scoring.

It felt like coming home, like this is what I should have been doing all along. People had often used the word 'cinematic' to describe my music, but like so many things, I didn't see it myself and never would have believed I could have been good enough to do that. That was for proper musicians.

Chris and I have since re-recorded 'No One To Thank Or Blame' with the film and closing credits in mind, and that version can be found on the *Together* album.

In the intervening years we have learned a huge amount about the film industry and the creative process of film scoring, but what struck me was how easily and readily I took to it. To be honest, I'd never really been interested in instrumental music – the lyric and the story had always been strong drivers for me creatively. But I found that creating moods with sounds and different combinations of instruments is incredibly fulfilling, much like the process I followed of creating 'No One To Thank', just letting my imagination build up a picture with sounds. Film work is also so very varied. Something that has been equally a blessing and a curse is that I can't stick to doing one thing.

Variety is what keeps me creatively fulfilled, and if I feel that I'm recycling the same ideas over and again, I become very dejected quite quickly, and question everything including my own purpose and existence.

So far we have been involved with a number of independent projects and built up a wonderful network of independent filmmakers. I really take my hat off to them. So many are so driven and passionate about their stories. It reminded me that I'm a storyteller, and taught me that I can tell stories in ways that don't necessarily use words. Depending on the film, I have been challenged to look at instruments and cultures that I would never have considered as a singer-songwriter. I've created things that really would have been too arty-farty for my singer-songwriter hat – church organ meets trip hop, oriental martial arts soundtracks, Taiko drums, harpsichords, Navajo Indian vocals... And it just goes on and on; I get swept away with it. It's a door I'm hoping will be open for a very long time. The projects are getting bigger and more exciting, and we're honing our skills and getting more creative with each opportunity.

Every now and then I have to remind myself that it all started with these four lines of lyric, and a tinker on my beaten-up piano. It pays to indulge your creativity sometimes and to hell with the consequences. Turns out they could be better than you ever dreamed they could be.

Track 2:
Rough With The Smooth

Blue under her eyes
Black on her feet
Wishing away with all her heart
Another working week
But she don't gamble
And she won't cheat
And she's got her man's kiss
There on her cheek

That day as the morning broke
As she raised her weary head
He squeezed her freezing fingers
And kissed her as he said

You gotta take the rough with the smooth
If you wanna hold on to what is true
Take the rough with the smooth
Darlin' me and you
You gotta take the rough with the smooth
And baby we'll make it through
We'll take the rough with the smooth
Darling me and you

Tear in his coat
Hole in his jeans
Wishing he could just work out
What the hell all this means
Why is nothing simple?
Or what it seems?
Except the way he loves his wife
And the way he shares her dreams

You gotta take the rough with the smooth
If you wanna hold on to what is true
Take the rough with the smooth
Darlin' me and you
You gotta take the rough with the smooth
And baby we'll make it through
We'll take the rough with the smooth
Darling me and you

This was drawing on my life experience of trying to 'settle down', something that so many people get such a huge amount of satisfaction from. After more than my fair share of globetrotting years, I started to settle into the world of work and do things that were on my 'to do' list, like 'grow up' and 'get a proper job'. Having been told years before that I couldn't be a singer – don't be so ridiculous – I set about trying to find something else constructive to do that would earn me enough money to buy a house. After my travelling I would have been very happy doing a range of charity work, but to earn a living didn't seem possible, certainly not where I was looking anyway. Out of almost desperation I went for a careers assessment with the local council and they found some things that might suit me. I picked something and thankfully got the job. Quickly I got myself some responsibilities, financial obligations and was well on the way to having a proper job and settling down. Sadly, I hated it. I felt trapped, unfulfilled, I was making not one bit of difference to anyone (or so I thought), and I wasn't even making enough money to live on really. Great. This song was about the feeling of responsibility I had to keep going, and the belief that I'd get my rewards in the long run.

I found some pockets of things that sparked my interest along the way, but the long and short of it was that I was fundamentally unfulfilled with the expectations I had at that point in my life, and the things that were expected of me.

Solace was found in music of course: writing, playing, performing. Over the years people have told me that they've related to this simple story about a young couple trying to find their place in the world. That's all an artist needs sometimes.

Track 3:
Nearby
For Geoffrey

Sometimes I feel closer to you
Even though you're further away
I feel you here, more than before
And I know that feeling will stay
I'm beginning to understand
What happened and where you've gone
I'm so glad I knew you
That we shared our little song

I was just a small part of your life
But I loved it, the memory too
You taught me something
By doing nothing but being you

I love the way that you are
And I loved the way you were
I'm so glad I knew you
I want to be the way you were

Our worlds won't separate us
I'll always hear you laugh in my heart
I know we can't be together
But we'll never be apart

For Geoffrey Ian Randell, 1st June 1976 – 19th February 1998, the first friend I ever made, at the age of two.

I don't think I realised until well after the fact that *Fearless* quite clearly reflects a difficult period in my life. Difficult things still happen of course, such is life, but now with wisdom and life experience perhaps I can be more philosophical about it. But what happened to Geoffrey was truly tragic.

I met Geoff when I was two, when my family moved in next door to his. He must have been about six and his sister was maybe eight years old, or even a bit bigger. My first memory of him, and one of my earliest memories at all, is of talking to him through the garden fence. One time when we were in his garden, with just pants and wellies on (not uncommon), he thought it would be a great idea to fill my wellies up with water. Compliantly, I stood there while he stuck the hose in each boot. I forget why, but at some point in the proceedings I said "I'm only three you know" for which he teased me for the rest of his life. We all had a chuckle for a bit… and then I tried to get them off. Nope. Geoff had got me stuck in my wellies and I couldn't get out. Still to this day I don't know why he did it, but we definitely bonded over this experience. I think it became the foundation of our relationship.

We stayed friends through school, and shared a tutor for a while who gave us extra classes outside of school. I remember her tales of trying to teach him exam technique, when at the beginning of the exam instead of counting the questions and working out how much time he had to spend on each problem, he would take his fountain pen to pieces and put it back together again. He had a daft daft daft sense of humour, and a laugh like Goofy that I will always 'hear in my heart'. We had a lovely friendship with a brotherly kind of protective tone, that occasionally was peppered with a very light flirtation when we were both older. He gave me confidence in myself because subconsciously I knew he saw me for the tender-hearted little soul I was. I was fat and had crooked teeth, for which I was bullied mercilessly at primary school. I felt ugly most of my childhood and formative years, and he was someone outside of my usual group of peers who made me feel better about myself. Maybe he knew I needed that. The occasional person would pass comment about us forming a romantic attachment, but we'd always respond with "Ewww gross". We were too close for that.

As we got older, I always asked him about important decisions – what did he think I should do, what was his opinion on this event or that thing that happened. He was always great to talk to and a wonderful listener. I can't help but think this could have featured in his chosen career somehow, had he the opportunity to have one. His advice was usually sensible and considerate – I don't know how many people would have chosen the word 'sensible' to describe him – but he always managed to say the right thing to me. I'm not sure the reverse is true. We were chatting outside the chippy in the village once, and he asked me what I thought about what kind of car he should get; he guffawed that goofy, bellowing laugh at my reply, "one with a roof rack". Apparently that wasn't helpful.

So Geoff got a car – a light coloured Morris Minor I believe – and it was all CB radios at the time. His handle was 'Captain Greenfingers', and the height of entertainment those days was to sit in the car with the CB radio and look for other people to talk to. Quite literally looking for people on the same wavelength. Sometimes I'd go with him but not often.

I must have been about 14 or 15 when he went off to university. After a while he got a Sunday job as a security guard for some building in Kingston where nothing ever happened. That in itself we used to laugh about because he was the most unlikely shape and temperament for that. He'd sit there by himself all day, bored out of his mind, so he'd phone people. We spent hours and hours on the phone when he had that job, talking about all manner of things, including details I'm sure his girlfriend wouldn't appreciate. He was meant to check in with the other guards on duty every now and then, but we'd get chatting and quite frequently we'd be interrupted by one of the others walking round to his desk to make sure he was ok.

During the holidays he'd come home. He scared my mum outside our house one night because she didn't know he was back, and in the intervening months, he'd grown a massive beard and bought himself a big black Garth Brooks hat. Excited to see my mum, he ran up to the car in the dark, but she didn't recognise him and locked all the car doors. He identified himself and all was well, but we all found it very funny for many years to come. Except maybe Mum. Poor Mum.

One of my greatest regrets is that the last time he called me, I didn't speak to him. I was just going out and I knew it wouldn't be a short conversation; it never was. That's one of those things I wish I could change. My memory of that time became that I'd seen him a few weeks before the accident, when he'd come home for Christmas and we'd bumped into each other at Midnight Mass. We'd been going to St Nicholas since we were tiny and both enjoyed some Christmas carols. It was a brief meeting; he was in the throes of his final year at uni and only come home for two days for Christmas. I was lucky, and subsequently very grateful, to have seen him that night. I'd believed the accident to have not been very long after that.

When I came to write this book, I reached out to Geoff's family to make sure they were happy with what I've said, and subsequently learned that the timeline of my memories was not quite right. I admit to feeling quite saddened by this, but you never really know what grief and the passage of time does to your memories. It turns out the accident was actually on the 15th of December the following year, on a Monday tea time, and perhaps I'd seen him in the November when he came home for his mum's birthday. To be completely honest, I don't remember whether I saw him in the November or not, such was the nature of our friendship. He never told me he was coming; he just popped round. As is so often the way when you lose someone, I wish I could go back in time and freeze frame all those memories in technicolour; alas, all we have is the dwindling embers of our recollection. However, in the wise words of Maya Angelou, "People will forget what you said, people will forget what you did, but people will never forget how you made them feel", and that is certainly true here. I will never forget that he made me feel happy, amused, important, valued, and – with the wisdom of hindsight – loved.

I don't remember how I found out or who told me but it was probably my mum. Geoff had been in a car accident. I remember nobody really knowing what had happened, at least that's what they told me. He wasn't killed outright, but was in intensive care, in a coma. Now aged 17, I wanted to go and see him, but it was deemed to be inappropriate for my own good. I've since learned that only two people outside the family saw him in hospital. For years I regretted not being able to tell him what he'd meant to me when there was an outside chance that he could have heard me. Still now I have a tendency to be overly demonstrative with my affection because of this. My good friend Beth (the one who took the photo for the *Fearless* album cover) said to me recently, in a different context, "You don't need to tell me that – I know already, and I'm sure he did too", which is comfort beyond measure.

Nine weeks I believe he was in intensive care. It trickled back to us that there had been talk of having to make the decision to turn off his life support, but that was decided against. In the end I believe it was pneumonia that took him. I answered the phone one night and was asked to pass on the message to my mum that he'd gone that morning. Everyone was out. I just fell to the kitchen floor and wept, I don't know how long for.

The next few weeks were a blur.

But I had this feeling that he was here.

The funeral was packed.

God only knows what it must have been like for his parents and his sister. I spent a lot of time in the practice rooms at college just crying and trying to comfort myself, which is when this song was born. This feeling that he was in the room was really strong for about a month; maybe that's what people mean when they say they feel someone watching over them. In the subsequent years, I've come to understand that's how I felt about our friendship when he was here. Like he was looking out for me, watching over me in his gentle and mellow way. Sitting in that practice room at college, I knew he wasn't there, but sometimes I felt closer to him even though he was further away.

I'd lost relatives before, but in the natural order of things. To be confronted with my mortality at such a young age, and knowing that there was so much Geoff didn't get to do, has shaped my life and continues to. I don't want to waste time, or take it for granted. He wanted to travel and do so much, but he never got the chance. I live my life to the full for us both.

Overwhelming grief took me to my tutor Tim one break time, and I told him what had happened. I think it was roughly a month after Geoff's passing, if memory serves me correctly. I was struggling to do anything, and that month felt like aeons.

Never having experienced anything like this, I heard myself say to Tim, exasperated, "I just want to get over it." Tim replied, "It's about learning to live with the pain." Over the years I've found ways of doing that. I still 'talk' to him and think about what he would have said if I'm struggling with a decision; I remember him fondly, think of him daily, and talk of him often. I'm grateful for all the ways my life is better because of him; he taught me to live my life to the full, which is the greatest lesson I have learned. Part of me is always that little three-year-old stuck in my red welly boots, happy as a clam.

Despite the number of people who have encouraged me to write this book, I struggled with it. I didn't want this body of work to be self-indulgent or egotistical, or indeed a biography. I procrastinated and talked myself in and out of it. Until I got to here. I realised that this was another opportunity to tell Geoff's story, another way I can show my gratitude for his love and friendship, and keep his memory alive. Once I realised that, I worked on it relentlessly. It makes me chuckle to myself because it's exactly what he would have said to my face. Get on with it, girl. He would have encouraged me to speak up proudly and share what I had to say, and not be afraid. His memory is still alive and encouraging me to be stronger, to be true to myself. Even though I still miss him every day and wish he was still here, that comforts me.

I tell his story to you, dear reader, in the hope that you might find some wisdom in it. Make the most of your time, and laugh like Goofy as often as you can.

Track 4:
No One Is Wise

*The days when you truly believe your
dreams will only lead to bad things
And you wanna fly but you know you ain't got no wings
So you stargaze a fantasy
But when you open your eyes you see what you always see*

*So when the rainbow's black and white and
the sun is dark as the moon at night
When only birds with no wings in flight and
the distant future is out of sight
Then those with no eyes, no heavy disguise, no shield of lies, tries
No wings, no one flies, no one is wise who thinks
they are the only ones who are right*

*The days when you truly believe you're always
gonna think but you'll never feel
And no matter how hard you try what
you want is never gonna be real
So you stargaze a fantasy
But when you open your eyes you see what you always see*

So when the rainbow's black and white and
the sun is dark as the moon at night
When only birds with no wings in flight and
the distant future is out of sight
Then those with no eyes, no heavy disguise, no shield of lies, tries
No wings, no one flies, no one is wise who thinks
they are the only ones who are right

Don't be fooled into thinking everybody
knows where they're going
Don't be fooled into thinking everybody
knows what they're doing
Don't be fooled into thinking everybody knows who they're lovin'
Don't be fooled into thinking everybody knows why they're cryin'
Coz they don't

So when the rainbow's black and white and
the sun is dark as the moon at night
When you're convinced that wrong is right and no
matter how hard you try, you're gonna lose the fight
Then open your eyes, shed your disguise,
undo your lies, you can always try
Spread your wings and fly, you can learn to be wise,
just open your mind and do what's right

As a philosophy student, I'd also come to realise that truth is a relative term, and depending on your point of view, two opposing opinions could be considered to be equally true.

'No One Is Wise' was a story about working out who to listen to, where I stood in the world, and what I stood for. Before writing songs, I started writing poetry when I was very young, and I love the indulgence of the poetic lyric in this track.

When I lived in Cardiff, I used to perform this with my acoustic trio The Juniper Berries. We enjoyed playing at acoustic showcases, covering artists we loved like Lindisfarne, Fleetwood Mac and Ryan Adams, as well as playing my original songs. 'No One Is Wise' always went down well at our shows and I always enjoyed performing it with Alex and Laura. This song was created during a time when you would gig the songs over and over before recording them, and the natural evolution of the piece would happen before it was recorded for all time.

I miss that to be truthful; it's much more the trend to record now and gig later, such are the advances in technology. Having said this, when I came to record it a few years later, inspired by the Eagles song 'Hole In The World' where different sections of the song are sung over each other, I tried it with 'No One Is Wise', as the guitar part is the same throughout. As it's just the melody that changes from verse to chorus to bridge, it stood to reason that they would create at least some harmony when sung together. I did this on my digital 8track in my bedroom, and was very pleased with myself, not realising I was making huge work for any act I performed with in the future.

We are yet to have perfected performing this section as it is, but it demonstrates to me how the recording process can liberate other creative ideas. When not limited by what is physically possible with whichever line-up of musicians I may currently be with, the song potentially takes on other colours. This has been an interesting balance for me as a creative, and depending on what phase I'm in as an artist, different things have been important to me. When making *Fearless* it was important to me that everything was real; all the instruments were played live and nothing was programmed. Raw and real.

'No One Is Wise' just happened to reflect that state of mind of being unsure of oneself, and having all those thoughts running through my mind simultaneously.

Track 5:
If She Believed In Heaven

A young girl kneeling under a spire
Trying to talk to the Lord
Her hands are folded but her eyes are open wide
Coz she can't feel a single word

Coz if she believed in heaven
If she believed in love
If she believed in heaven
She wouldn't be feeling like hell

An old man resting next to the fire
Trying to warm through his soul
The war is distant but the cries are far too close
Coz he can hear them every morn

Coz if he believed in heaven
If he believed in love
If he believed in heaven
He wouldn't be feeling like hell

Coz if we believed in heaven
If we believed in love
If we believed in heaven
We wouldn't be feeling like hell

This song is a culmination of several things really. Firstly, let me tell you where I was when I wrote it. A fairly full first draft came to me backstage, whilst waiting to play at an artists' showcase in Bristol. For some reason I was there extremely early – if memory serves me correctly I had been performing in another band at a festival earlier in the day. People used to 'get me in' for backing vocals and percussion on their larger gigs, to fill out the band and layer up harmonies. While I was in town, I had also been booked as a solo artist later that evening. I quite enjoy enforced hanging around if I'm comfortable and left in peace. My life is so hectic most of the time, these pockets of peace can be oases of creativity, particularly as a solo artist. Nowadays we tend to head to a bar or a restaurant, to be honest, or have a collective nap in the dressing room. Rock and roll!

I was all full of melody and some bits of lyric loitering in my mind. Songbook in hand, as always, I started to scribble away. Originally the line was 'freewheeling to hell', which I'm grateful to say mellowed to a metaphorical 'feeling like hell'; I do like to squeeze in an everyday saying where I can. It's something relatable that I've heard lots of people say. Although I forget the specifics, this was in some way a response to a verse in 'Redemption Song', one of my regular Bob Marley covers, that talks about freeing ourselves from the limitations of our own thinking. That song was bound to have been in my set that night. In 'Redemption Song', Bob Marley talks about the desperately sad history of his people and how he found strength in his religion.

Religion had always fascinated me. I'd studied it keenly from a young age and asked many probing questions during my travels, asking to be taken to places and events of religious significance. But the blind faith in something bigger... I was always jealous of that. What a comfort it must be in dark times. When Geoff died, I found myself hoping that his heaven that he was so deserving of came true for him. Agnostic little me just making the best of what I have now.

During my studies, one of the main arguments people made against the existence of God was our mania for war. These disjointed thoughts manifested themselves into the verses, each a tableau of a different story for a different character.

One of the things that struck me when studying and investigating religion is just how much they all have in common: Judaism, Christianity, Buddhism, Islam, Jainism, Hinduism, Sikhism – when you strip them to the core, they are really saying the same things. Be nice to each other. As nice as you can. To the average person in the street, we could call that love. That's a concept that transcends culture, upbringing, religion, atheism and circumstances. We might disagree on how to do it, but love is something most people understand, and the theme I chose for the chorus.

When we came to revisit this song to perform it in the era of my latest album, the last chorus underwent a very small amendment. When we sing this live now, the last chorus is "if we believe in love..." which to me demonstrates a bit more of a solution to our trials and tribulations.

Track 6:
Time Will Heal

Years pass
Hours last

Time moves on, right or wrong,
Until the hurt is gone
Time will heal

Hands shake
Hearts break

Time moves on, right or wrong,
Until the hurt is gone
Time will heal

Birds fly, children cry
We all live with some grey skies
Birds fly, oceans dry in time
Time will heal

Hearts break
Hands shake

Time moves on, right or wrong,
Until the hurt is gone
Time will heal
Time will heal

In contrast to some of my other pieces, 'Time Will Heal' is lyrically sparse. I wrote the guitar part first, which actually did not make it onto the *Fearless* recording. However, in the years between writing and recording it, I'd been tinkering with the pretty guitar part and originally the song started life as a lullaby. During my darker years, sleep and I were not happy bedfellows. I suffered terrible insomnia for years. The lullaby was an attempt to creatively rock myself to sleep. Perhaps it didn't work because I didn't really believe it? Unhappy with the saccharine, twee nature of the lyric, I never really did anything with it in that incarnation. Instinctively I knew that the lyric was not as robust as the musical elements of the song.

On the road again a few years later, I found myself playing it in the garden of the guesthouse I was staying at during my travels visiting a charity in Madagascar. I always travelled with a small guitar at that time, sometimes mistaken for a tennis racquet. This amused me no end, as the thought of me playing tennis at all is just laughable, let alone enough to take a racquet with me everywhere I go. Still, I guess not everyone agrees with that. Somewhere, there is an old dictaphone recording of me playing this against the din of the evening Malagasy crickets.

Thinking back to the conversation with Tim, I realised that I had started to feel better, and although some of the pain would never go away, I was living a life of purpose. I'd lose people and meet new people throughout my life, and being open to that would bring me more fulfilment. Not yet fully cognizant of how losing Geoffrey had begun to shape me, I was living. I was functioning. I was taking advantage of the opportunities still available to me. My trip to Madagascar had involved me taking part in the training of some of the volunteers for a charity based there; I was excited to be involved, to be of use, and to go to such a remote country by myself. Freedom. Living life to the full.

In 2019 I re-recorded this as a single with my original guitar part, and simplified backing vocals, which was a more contemporary sound at the time of recording. That made it suitable for representation by one of our agents in Los Angeles, who loved the arrangement, original guitar part and the message.

Many songs, cultures, religions and mums say "This too will pass". 'Time Will Heal' is my version of that.

I guess you could say in many situations that time does heal. What I've learned is that the trick is knowing what to do with yourself in the meantime.

Track 7:
Painted Sails

I lost you on the seas of change
Tried to lift you out of harm's way
Now you drifted so far away
Just come on home to me
On Painted Sails

I've been foolish and I've been naïve
And I guess I heard only what I wanted to believe
Now I just wanna know baby how long you'll be
Just come on home to me
On Painted Sails

Show me another way to hurry you home
Don't make me break another shore along
Show me another way to hurry you along
To come on home to me
On Painted Sails

No I'm hoping those tides of change will be kind
And you'll bring back my little sailboat with my heart inside
You'll be on board with three little words set aside
Just come on home to me
On Painted Sails
On Painted Sails

This song features my dear friend Pete Hartley on strings, and he always said he could hear a gospel quality in this track. It's funny because that's not what I would have said, but I did write it in a beautiful church in Southsea whilst waiting to start a gospel workshop I was leading many years ago. I was waiting for my singers to arrive and just sat down in this beautiful space at the delicious grand piano. This particular church is a traditional stone and marble building and the acoustics are incredible. Uncharacteristically, I was very early for some reason, and I just sat down and started playing. I fiddled around with the seed of an idea I had been playing with and wrote this pretty quickly.

This song structure is called 'jazz standard format' where there is no chorus. You have to find your repetition somewhere else, and the structure is very compact. Many of Carole King's hits are written in this format, and I find it a lovely structure to work within.

At the time I sat down at the piano, I was once again in a relationship I knew was breaking down. In songwriting terms, this is called an 'autumn love song'. Unaware of all the facts at the time, I was hoping against hope that we'd resolve things, but I knew something was seriously wrong. I was scared and I was desperate. The first draft was really quite depressing, and I'm grateful to Pete for giving it a positive lift. This has enabled me to look back on this song with fondness.

It's taken on another meaning to me now, since I know that relationship breaking down was for the absolute best. 'Painted Sails' now carries a message of being separated from somebody you love, but their absence making your heart grow fonder. Excitement that they'll be back soon, and celebration, impatience for your reunion. Without Pete's interpretation – perhaps he heard that at the time – I don't think I could enjoy this song as I do now.

Track 8:
I Knew An Angel

I knew an angel all my life
She spoke my dreams in rhyme
She showed me pathways, love and strife
But now she's lost in time

And heaven needs her where she has gone
And when she comes back home I'll be where I belong
I knew an angel all my life
But she's in heaven now

I knew an angel, the stars, moon, sun
She said sink, swim or drown
Look inside you, there's always one
Who's gonna let you down

And heaven bleeds her where she has gone
And when she comes back home I'll be where I belong
Where I belong

In the midst of turmoil and confusion and hurt, this song appeared. In poetry, my feelings of grief and confusion over my place in the world came together. Taking my place in the adult world was scary as well as exciting, and at times I felt lost and disappointed. When I didn't know what to do with myself, I wondered if I had a destiny, if there was a plan, or if someone was watching over me. There was a feeling that I always knew something special was waiting for me but I'd been hurt and let down, bereaved and heartbroken. Deep down I knew I had to make my own destiny, but was mustering the strength to find it.

There is love and hope in this lyric, but the disappointed love and fragile hope of an insecure young woman.

Track 9:
Fearless

You remind me of getting my heart broke
You remind me of dreamin' before I woke
You reminded me of words that I never spoke

You remind me of how to not be afraid
How to get to the places where dreams are made
You reminded me to step out of the shade

Coz it's fear that holds people in their madness
And it's fear that holds people in their darkness
But it's clear
You make me fearless

Now I know you gotta be on your way
But the lesson is here to stay
If the picture isn't perfect doesn't mean that you throw it away

Coz it's fear that holds people in their madness
And it's fear that holds people in their darkness
But it's clear
You make me fearless yeah yeah
Fearless yeah yeah
Ooh

Coz it's fear that holds people in their madness
And it's fear that holds people in their darkness
Baby it's clear
You make me fearless
Fearless
Fearless

The title track of this album, 'Fearless' is one of those songs that just came through me. Sometimes it feels like another energy is moving through me when a song is created. After a few years of difficulty I knew I'd turned a corner. I was losing the anger and the edge of 'No One To Thank Or Blame' although these two songs were both written in a similar time frame. Coming up for air after a suffocating relationship, finally resurfacing after a nasty separation that had made me question everything, I was starting to feel myself again. I had allowed myself to get lost in the murky, unrealistic desires of a destructive relationship that would have killed me if I didn't get out. Leaving was terrifying but the time came where I couldn't give any more of myself. An amazing lesson to learn at such a young age.

Don't give all of yourself to a dark situation expecting to find the light; your light is inside you and you need to nourish that part of yourself to truly be alive. The natural assumption is that 'Fearless' is a love song, but it was more than that to me. It was looking at the concept of love, the ideals of being alive, the possibilities of dreams yet to be realised, the thrill of the chase, the journey, the joy, the lessons learned to take forward.

I knew the fear had stopped me moving forward and kept me trapped in a dark place for a long time. Even when I didn't know what I was afraid of. Doubting everything and feeling stuck in a life I didn't want. At times during that period I felt like my life was already over. I'd had my time for enjoying life. Breaking that belief and coming through the other side felt like stepping back into the sunshine. The song 'Fearless' flowed through me onto my piano when I was ready to shake off the shackles and take centre stage in my own life again.

I knew it was a strong song. Like most of my work, when I'm at my most vulnerable and genuine, the song has a life of its own.

When it came to recording it, I knew that I wanted to ask Pete to play strings for me, but I'd never played my own piano parts in the studio before. Preferring to defer to other people who I felt knew better than me, I'd never felt good enough to do it. But it was a simple enough part, it's honest, it's as it came through me, and it was time for me to be brave. I am more proud of this song than I could have ever imagined; when I heard the first mix with Pete's luscious strings, I knew my new life had started. This was me. This was the sort of song I'd dreamed of putting my name to all my life. Pete brings a new level of experience to a song – listen to the pizzicato plucks in the verse "you remind me of how to not be afraid" – he plays the message in the lyric and enhances it. It's a beautiful collaboration.

'Fearless' was a milestone for me as a new chapter of my life started, as a shining light of a song that flew my flag as an artist, and something I am exceptionally proud of.

Track 10:
Don't Want To Fight

It's the middle of the night
I've got no more fight
I couldn't say who was right
Anymore
We both tried so hard
Though I never let down my guard
I just can't keep up the charade
Anymore

But I still remember those perfect days even
though we've gone our separate ways
I understand that you wanna settle the score
And I could force the sun to shine if I
could just turn back the time
But I just don't wanna fight anymore

I feel like an empty train
Ploughing through the rain
I can't have this same fight again
Anymore
There is no other guy
But you're determined that's a lie
I just don't understand why
Anymore

But I still remember those perfect days even
though we've gone our separate ways
I understand that you wanna settle the score
And I could force the sun to shine if I
could just turn back the time
But I just don't wanna fight anymore

It's late at night
I got no more fight
I just don't know who's right
Our dreams have broke in two
I don't belong with you
And I know you feel it too

But I still remember those perfect days even
though we've gone our separate ways
I understand that you wanna settle the score
And I could force the sun to shine if I
could just turn back the time
But I just don't wanna fight anymore

I just don't wanna fight anymore

We've probably all been in a relationship where we're sick of having the same arguments over and over again. Be that work, family, a partner. In songwriting terms, this is a 'winter love song', the end of a relationship and everyone is hurting.

This is a more acoustic version of one of my most popular songs with the pop/rock band. The electric guitar hints back to that era. Having this track on *Fearless* was important to me, because of what it nearly did for us as a pop/rock group. Although I always knew in my heart I wasn't a rock artist, I let myself get lured into someone else's opinion that commerciality was more important than artistic integrity. A large record company heard the rock version of this track and asked for a simple rewrite, but my personal relationship had broken down so much that this never got done, as my partner at the time was also the producer.

No matter what I did, he wouldn't book the band into the studio. The record company lost interest. Considering it was the producer's decision to push for commercial viability, I was heartbroken that we'd lost this opportunity because of our own shortcomings. I've missed opportunities, I've had things go wrong, but never because I'd lain down and quit before, and I felt I'd let that happen this time. It stung for a long time.

Having a new incarnation of 'Don't Want To Fight' on *Fearless*, alongside new songs, helped me let go of that anger and take ownership of the song back. As it happens, had I been signed to this big label back then, I wouldn't have the artistic freedom I have now, so on balance I have nothing to regret, despite the stinging.

Album: *Together*
Released: 07/04/2018

This is another figment of my imagination brought to life by the fantastic digital artist Lauren Norton. Lauren is also the artist for the singles 'Already A Hero', 'In The Bleak Midwinter' and 'Strong'.

In contrast to *Fearless*, I wanted *Together* to be bright, colourful and detailed. The tree in the centre is a picture of a tree that is near where I live. It's in the middle of some farmer's fields and I just love that it has never been cut down. It's a beautiful shape, and as I see it nearly every time I go out, I watch it change with the seasons. When I see the Together Tree I know I'm nearly home. If you look closely, the tree also represents two people embracing.

Bringing together a variety of different styles on this album, I had the idea of the animals all suggesting a circle, implying all walks of life moving together. Lauren did an incredible job of making my ideas a reality. The colours are so vivid and the detail so intricate. This image is also the same one that's used for the backdrop of our theatre show, such was the detail Lauren used – two metres by three metres and the image was still sharp and clear. *Together* is an eclectic shiny celebration of all of my accomplishments. Lauren reflected that.

Track 1:
Here With Me

Well it's rolling on to winter and summer's long since dead
I done wrapped up all the sunshine and left it home in bed but
I don't wanna know if you say you're gonna go if it's not
Here with me

Coz I know that you been lonely and you know that I have too
But there'll always be a place here, my love
you know that's true, it's just
I don't wanna know if you say you're gonna go if it's not
Here with me

Coz baby it's not easy when you have to go away
But they say home is where your heart is
so you better come home safe
And I'll always just be restless till you're resting by my face

Now the nights are getting longer and cold is drawing in
But when I'm safe in your embrace it doesn't
matter where we been, now
All I really know when you say you've gotta go you'll be back
Here with me
Baby you'll be back, baby you'll be back,
Here with me

Despite how the opening line of this lyric reads, this song, to me, is a happy one. Finding our place in the world can be terrifying, whether that's finding a partner, finding a purpose in life, fulfilment in work, as a parent or within your own family. This song 'Here With Me' was an acknowledgement of the anxious feelings around not having a place, and the relief we feel when everything is right with the world.

This was the first song I wrote in earnest after *Fearless* was released. My struggle had been so real with *Fearless* that it had left me creatively bare. I started to have a horrible feeling that I'd burnt my creativity out of myself and I'd never have a good idea again. Artists of all kinds suffer these crippling doubts but I'd never felt it so keenly before.

I'd started recording with a new label in London who had expressed interest in the *Fearless* album, and I met a fab producer, James Arter, who I took to immediately. We'd recorded 'The Nesting Song' and 'Shelter From The Storm' together, which had been a lot of fun and we'd got on well. But even through this process, I hadn't had any urge to write and was starting to get quite worried. Who am I without my creativity? I still cannot answer that question.

Muddling along with the gazillion other things artists have to concern themselves with, I found myself going to a masterclass with a producer we knew. Now, you may laugh at this. This masterclass was about how to program digital drum patterns and was by Mark Hill, the man who invented UK garage. I'm very fond of Mark and the masterclass was really interesting, but I even said to him at the time that is about the last thing I would do to start writing. Program drums. Nope. I'm all about the story, the lyric, singable melodies, real instruments, raw human emotion, touch and feel. Not electronic drums. At least that's how I felt at the time. That doesn't make it invalid as an approach, and of course is integral to some genres of music, but it wasn't something I ever saw myself doing. Of course, that is no longer true, and many of our projects have begun with finding a good groove!

But something about being around other creative people nudged me that night. I came home and just sat at the piano playing with no agenda. I tinkered, flicked through some books and played some things I like to play on the piano, just amusing myself. Then before I knew what was happening, my dusty songbook was open and I was scribbling away. I tentatively floated the idea to James and he loved the demo I sent him. It was released that year as my Christmas single, and eventually became the first song on *Together*.

I was so pleased with it that we went on to make a full-blown music video for the single which was also great fun, as I got to dress up and be surrounded by twinkly lights backstage at one of my favourite theatres.

The lesson for me is that losing faith can be a self-fulfilling prophecy, I think. Once I felt I'd lost it, I stopped trying. And where does that get us, eh?

Track 2:
Take Care Of You

Do do do do, do do do do, do do do do, do do do do,
Take care of you
Do do do do, do do do do, do do do do, do do do do,
Take care of you

You're sweet just like an apple, sharp just like a pear,
And when you need a squeeze you know that I'll be there
When you need a friend, find me anywhere
To take care of you

Do do do do, do do do do, do do do do, do do do do,
Take care of you
Do do do do, do do do do, do do do do, do do do do,
Take care of you

You're sweet just like an angel, innocent and fair
And when you need some love you know that I'll be there
When you need a friend you'll find me anywhere
To take care of you

The ukulele was on the rise and I'd been playing it for quite a long time as an afterthought to guitar, really. The cultural shift to playing pop songs on ukulele had been happening for some years, and it seemed every pub had a strum along. It has taken much longer than that for ukulele to get back into popular music, but at the time of writing, it is becoming more and more popular amongst young female indie artists.

When I wrote 'Take Care Of You' I was having a bit of a love affair with a particular smoothie company I was very fond of. I'd followed their brand since its inception, and loved the example they had set for the commercial world. Everything was ethically sourced, long before it was fashionable; they had a chat line for exactly that – chatting – if you felt a bit lonely. They gave huge amounts of their profits to charity and everything was fair trade. It was everything my inner idealistic hippy loved. I had actually applied for a job to work there during my period of disillusionment with my 'proper job' but I lived too far away. The job had been to answer the phone (shaped like a piece of fruit), manning the special line published for people to call when they were lonely. I loved that this big corporation had such a heart. 'Take Care Of You' was written on ukulele to reflect the whimsical tone of the company, and filled with fruity imagery. It was a bit of fun, and I very much enjoyed getting my family in on gang vocals for that sing along sound.

Track 3:
Shelter From The Storm

For Isobelle

The first time your mother heard you laughing
The first time your daddy saw you cry
Open up your eyes and see the sunshine
We dreamed of all the things you'd ever try

And we'll do our best to shelter you from every storm
Wrap you up and keep you safe and warm
Show you all the love and strength and courage
That arrived the day that you were born

Each time a cloud becomes a castle
Each time you learn something new
Every time your soul is touched with wonder
Our hearts and souls will be touched too

And on those days when the sun won't shine
We'll be on our way, put your hand in mine

And we'll do our best to shelter you from every storm
Wrap you up and keep you safe and warm
Show you all the love and strength and courage
That arrived the day that you were born

'Shelter From The Storm' revisited

Several years ago, as you know, a very close friend of mine, Kate, had a baby and asked me to be godparent, a huge honour. As I mentioned in the song's first incarnation on *Beautiful Monday*, it was a simple lullaby for a tiny, beautiful, magical baby.

Having written this song when Isobelle was very new, I remember wondering what she would make of it when she was old enough to understand it. When it came to recording the track for *Beautiful Monday*, it was rushed, like all the tracks were because we were so pushed for time. Although I wasn't unhappy with the simplicity of the original, it always felt like unfinished business to me.

The original version has now been played and performed at baby naming ceremonies and christenings around the world, and I could not have foreseen its popularity. Parents and godparents have bought the sheet music and performed it themselves and it has been very popular with new mums. I'm thrilled that so many families relate to how I felt when Isobelle was born. It's really very humbling.

2015 saw me in the studio with my new producer James Arter, under agreement to record two new singles with this studio. We agreed to record one completely new song ('The Nesting Song') and a new recording of an old song. Amidst a huge case of studio burnout, I was reluctant to enter into this agreement, but it was necessary to record new tracks.

This way boundaries could be maintained between their input into work I undertook with them and my back catalogue which I had completed on my own. Otherwise it's difficult to discern who should be credited, and therefore paid, for any success any one song might see. Exhausted from decision making, I gave James my entire back catalogue and let him choose. Out of them all, he chose 'Shelter From The Storm'.

I was absolutely delighted to have the time, and expertise, to give this song the love it deserved, and it got me excited about being in the studio again. On the day we came to record vocals, I was actually at the end of a five-day sugar and caffeine detox, and my voice was moving so smoothly. James is a vocalist too and it was wonderful to have a producer who shared my passion for harmonies and backing vocals. Those two things conspired to see me standing in the vocal booth in the dark (just because that's how I like it!) for about two hours, and I just sang and sang. I sang my little heart out.

Shelter From The Storm single artwork

It feels that this version was sung more about the parents' experience, emblematic of the flood of emotions and maturation that accompany becoming a parent, rather than the sweet lullaby to soothe a newborn baby as it was in its original form.

I did get the opportunity to sit down with Isobelle that year with the original recording and watch her listen to it; this was an amazing experience now that she was old enough to understand it.

The new recording was released on 1st of December 2015 as my first ever Christmas single. Because I'd had so many requests for the music for people to use it themselves, when we released the new version, I also made the backing track available for people to use for their own ceremonies.

After the release, we came up with the idea of shooting a video with Isobelle in it. She was old enough now to be able to take a little direction and understand what was going on. We had a great day and Belle did really well. Filming can be quite intense, but she took it all in her stride, cutely making daisy chains and skipping around in the field with me. It was a very proud moment; I enjoyed the process immensely, and we will both always have that special time captured in Glen Jevon's most beautiful videography.

I was so happy that so many people related to how I felt when Isobelle was born, and I feel it cemented our bond. It's been a real privilege to show Isobelle what an inspiration she has been to so many people around the world. Including her own godmother.

Track 4:
Pink Champagne

We're at a junction and the lights are green
I can see from where we are
We're gonna have the things we've never seen
And boy we've come so far
We always knew we'd make it, just have a little faith coz

We're gonna celebrate a brand new day
Come on and share a glass of pink champagne
Oh oh oh oh oh we're ready for this change

We're on the road and the coast is clear
It's a beautiful scene
Our hopes are high and our dreams are near
And everything between
We always knew we'd make it, just have a little faith coz

We're gonna celebrate a brand new day
Come on and share a glass of pink champagne
We won't let anyone get in our way
We're gonna celebrate a brand new day
Oh oh oh oh oh we're ready for this change

We always knew we'd make it, just have a little faith coz

We're gonna celebrate a brand new day
Come on and share a glass of pink champagne
We won't let anyone get in our way
We're gonna celebrate a brand new day
We'll work our butts off and we won't complain
We're gonna celebrate, celebrate a brand new day
Oh oh oh oh oh we're ready for this change

We're ready for this
We're ready for this
We're ready for this
We're ready
Oh oh oh oh oh we're ready for this change

'Pink Champagne' was the culmination of several ideas. I was getting excited about the film work; the projects we were getting involved with getting more and more elaborate. Our studio was pretty new, which was a lifetime dream of mine. I also had always wanted a 'booze' song, having been pipped at the post for a song called 'Rosé' years ago, by a band called The Feeling. Funnily enough I wrote the lyrics to 'Pink Champagne' at a silent retreat with Sheryl Andrews and Karen Williams, my booky friends. On the exterior I was silent, but in my head I was singing this! A few lyrics were created that day, but only 'We'll Be Home' and 'Pink Champagne' have made it to completion so far.

We like a pink bubbly, and while the studio was all mine to experiment with to my heart's content, I spent about an hour trying to tune two empty bottles of bubbly! That 'dink donk' you can hear through the track is me playing the champagne bottles!

Track 5:
The Nesting Song

It's been a while now since I fell in love with you
We've been around now and lived in a place or two
But it's time now to just sit down and stay
So baby bricks and mortar, it's the only way

So let's buy ourselves a little house and decorate the hall
We'll find all the things broken and then we'll slowly fix them all
But in time now we'll put some pictures on the walls
And just be together behind our own front door

And you'll have me even when your day is long
And me, I'll never be alone
And maybe in time we'll put some little people down the hall
And just be together behind our own front door

It's been a while now since you fell in love with me
But baby I'll be yours eternally

And I'll have you even when my day is cold
And at night we can keep each other warm
And maybe in time we'll put some little people down the hall
And just be together behind our own front door

It's been a while now since I fell in love with you
We've been around now and lived in a place or two
But it's time now to just sit down and stay
So baby bricks and mortar, it's the only way

This is a happy, upbeat song about the greatest adventure we embark upon – building relationships. This is dedicated to all my friends who fell in love and were brave enough to build a life for themselves, taking a risk on another person, and is inspired by my friend Naomi when she bought a house with her husband. They'd moved around a bit from city to city and settled in Edinburgh. They were both happy as happy can be about it, and I was so pleased for them.

When Naomi told me the news I was playing a gig on the Music Train just outside Bristol, and I wrote the first verse and chorus on the way home. It stayed in my songbook, loitering for a while. When I was recording with James Arter in London he encouraged me to finish it, and we recorded it. I had got a bit stuck with where to take it, and started casting around for things to jog my creativity. I bought a 'home' magazine, and read some of the articles, underneath pictures of luxuriously dressed dining room tables, opulent Christmas decorations and deep pile carpets.

Whilst I had not seen their particular house, I thought to myself that this is not what happens when you first have a house. Things are broken, they need fixing, when you fix one thing, something else becomes apparent and it's a slow jigsaw piece of building a home together, and that's the metamorphosis that makes it yours. That thought helped me finish the picture in my head and bring the song to life: "We'll find all the things broken and then, slowly fix them all". Later, Naomi told me, "Your line about DIY is spot on for our experience – we felt like we were trapped inside 'The Gasman Cometh'", a very funny Flanders and Swann song reflecting the cyclical nature of home improvements. At the time of writing, they are still in the same house that they adore, loving life and winning competitions for growing sunflowers in the garden.

Track 6:
Already A Hero

Standing tall
A darkness that becomes a light
A hope that gets us through the night
Taking a chance
Together we are strong

Walk this road
Grateful for who came before
With the courage to explore
We are afraid
Together we are strong

Already a hero
Still holding strong
Already a hero
Though the ride may be long

Leave behind
A legacy for those to come
Let them know they're not alone
We all need a friend
Together we are strong

Already a hero
Still holding strong
Already a hero
Though the ride may be long
Already a hero
Still holding strong
Coast to coast, hear the bell ringing
Earth to sky, hear the singing
Already a hero

Oooh ooh

Already a hero
Still holding strong
Already a hero
Though the ride may be long
Already a hero
Still holding strong
Coast to coast, hear the bell ringing
Earth to sky, hear the singing
Already a hero

Already a hero
Already a hero
Already a hero
Already a hero

It's 2017, I am five months a newlywed, married to the love of my life and step-mum to Chris's beautiful daughter Caitlin, who was 14 when we got married.

Caity was her dad's 'best man' or 'best bird' as we called it, in honour of her Essex heritage on her father's side. Our wedding breakfast was small, with just 11 members of close family. My close friend Beth (the *Fearless* photographer) took our photos for us.

Caity and me on my wedding day

At the wedding breakfast, Caity gave a speech that floored every one of us. Penned entirely by her, it was about her struggles with her parents being separated when she was so small, and how her dad could have just walked away, but he didn't. To me, she said this:

"Family isn't to do with blood, it's the people in your life who accept you for who you are, do anything to see you smile, and love you no matter what. You may not have given me the gift of life, but you gave me the gift of you."

A luckier step-mum I cannot imagine.

That was in October 2016. On Boxing Day I noticed she was not really herself, and by the end of January I knew in the pit of my stomach something was seriously wrong. Because we'd had such a small ceremony, we had a big party for friends and family late the following January, and we all put our wedding clothes back on. Caity's dress was a lace-up back, and when tying it, I noticed it was hanging off her. I knew for a fact that that dress had fit her perfectly in October – I had my wedding photos to prove it. As it was such a beautiful dress, Beth had taken dozens of photos of her looking like a mystical princess.

I felt sick. Looking back now I wish I'd just taken her to A&E there and then. In my wedding dress. I don't have many regrets, but that is one of the few.

We went to our wedding reception and I started to convince myself maybe the weight loss wasn't that bad; she was a teenager and weird things happen to their bodies. At the party, Beth had all the photos flicking round for everyone to view, and the one of the back of Caity's dress popped up. Conspiratorially, I said to Beth "See, that dress did fit her, I'm not going mad." Ever full of good advice, Beth suggested I talk to Caity if I was worried. So I did, and I said that she needed to get her mum to take her to the doctor. Perhaps I could have been more emphatic about it, but I didn't want to frighten her. Either way, nothing happened. Caity got paler, more nauseous, off her food, faint and anxious. We were seeing her pretty infrequently then, with infrequent phone calls where she could not speak freely. Each time she was due to see us, we'd hope that she would be feeling better, but it just got worse and worse.

Caity and Chris's birthdays fall at the end of February and early March. The weekend in between just so happened to be our weekend to have her, so I planned a fun-packed weekend away in London for us as a family. They both love history, so we had tickets for the Tower of London, and my close friend

James Morgan was working at the BBC, and had offered us a tour. Caity's aunty and cousin came to meet us for the BBC tour and for dinner. Good fun was expected all round.

We had a little self-catering apartment on one side of London and were on the tube to meet Chris's sister Kerry and his niece Lauren. Caity was overcome with heat and nausea, and we had to get off the train at Oxford Street. She was pale and scared and horribly anxious. Doing the first thing I could think of, I ran up to the street to see what shops were around. Holland and Barrett was staring me in the face, so I went in and bought every vitamin tablet and product I could think of that might make her feel better. One of those things was a drink, and I think the faster absorption did make her feel a bit better that evening. She also knew deep down that something was wrong, and was asking her dad all manner of questions about what it might have been. But she perked up a bit, and managed some dinner. Between the drink and the dinner, I think it gave her the energy to enjoy James's tour and by the time we went back to the apartment she said she felt better than she had done in months. We thought we'd cracked it.

The following day was awful. We traipsed around the Tower of London monosyllabically. Caity was pale and anxious and nauseous. She ate nothing but a roast chicken flavoured packet of crisps, one crisp at a time, staring into the distance. It was awful. Her dad and I both knew something was wrong. The only ray of sunshine was when they both sang the 'Kings and Queens' song from *Horrible Histories*, drawing smiles from other parents who knew it.

We went home.

The little Trojan sat 10 days of mock exams starting the following day. With her anxiety through the roof, her teacher Mrs Burden sat with her at lunchtimes and made sure she ate something, offering her comfort and a safe space, for which I will always be grateful. As soon as her exams were over Caity had a doctor's appointment to receive some blood test results. It was a Wednesday. The doctor calmly sent her to the hospital, telling her to take a bag. We weren't with her.

Chris got a text message from her step-dad telling him she was in hospital. He'd get a call from the consultant later.

We were working. The call came.

"They think my daughter has cancer."

They were right.

The following week was probably the worst of my life. And whilst I don't like to speak for other people, it probably was for Chris and Caity too.

I believe in my heart that the time will come when Caity will tell you her story herself, but I know she had mixed feelings about the following weeks. It was the first time all four of her parents had been in the same place, and the first time her mum and dad had both sat by her bedside for as long as she could remember.

Thursday, Chris went to pieces, but I was strong for him. Caity was still on the children's ward. They moved her to oncology later that day. Friday, I went to pieces and Chris was strong for me. Caity had a biopsy that day. She'd had contrast tests, blood tests, blood transfusions, and words like lymphoma and leukaemia had been thrown around. Whilst they had alluded to what was wrong, we didn't have an official diagnosis. She was meant to go down in the morning so we would have had results by the end of the day, but an emergency pushed it back so she didn't go down until the afternoon. Being a Friday that meant we'd have to wait.

That Saturday Chris and I had a big event with our choir that was a big deal for us all. We'd been planning and training for it for weeks, but it looked like Chris was going to have to miss it. Usually, I would not share our personal troubles with our clients, but we had no choice as this now affected them. They were amazing, and rallied round for us.

We survived the weekend with some wonderful people around us. There's a song about that too.

The following three weeks Caity spent in hospital. We juggled work and visits and hospital appointments. One day while hanging around on the ward, Chris, sucker punched, was staring into space, I think wondering what on earth had hit us, and a lady called Nicola approached him. She was a social worker for a charity called CLIC Sargent who support families of children with cancer. She became a lifeline to us during Caity's treatment and the CLIC Sargent team became a key ingredient to keeping us on our feet during that time.

Caity was incredibly brave. She doesn't see it herself, but she was. Six rounds of chemotherapy, 11 rounds of radiotherapy with no complaints. She lost her long thick luscious hair and broke her leg when her bones became frail later on during her chemotherapy. She studied for the remainder of her last GCSE year by herself for the most part.

I could tell you the rest of our story, but this is the song's story. Before I go on, I want to tell you Caity beat it, thankfully is now in remission and at the time of writing, setting the world alight with her diligence, her beauty, her creativity, her passion, kindness and love.

During her treatment, we were separated from Caity for huge amounts of time. Once she left the hospital we could only see her infrequently and for short periods of time. CLIC Sargent were a key point of contact, keeping us informed about various aspects of her treatment – a real lifeline. Music has always been my therapy, and 'Already A Hero' was spilling out in awe of the amazing kids we had met along the way. Wanting to see the light in this situation, I went looking for it. I wanted the song to be uplifting, and a celebration of the bravery that everyone finds when the chips are seriously down. People said to us time and again "I don't know how you coped"; to be honest, neither do we. Only looking back on it I can see the things that kept us going, and the incidents that gave us hope. In truth we were doing everything we could to be strong for Caity and to put a smile on her face when we saw her. I was humbled by the bravery of her and the other kids on the ward and I wanted to express that they were all heroes to me, regardless of the outcome. Caity tells us that when the consultant told her she had cancer, her first question was "Am I going to die?" "I can't promise" was the reply. To be told that at 15 years old, in my opinion, meant the next inhale she took was a heroic act. And that is true of every child that goes through that experience. All the kids were dealing with it better than the adults by a country mile.

You may have noticed that there are no personal pronouns in the lyric. I did not want to pinpoint any particular point of view, because these situations are full of heroes. The medical staff, all the patients and researchers who had come before us to create the treatment that saved her life. There is so much to celebrate. On the ward there is a bell called the 'end of treatment bell'; this is another charity that gives kids something to look forward to. When declared officially in remission, the kids can ring the bell and everyone comes out into the corridor applauding. Caity was also given some money as a gift from the charity when she did it, which she put towards her amazing prom dress. She was just about recovered enough to go, and it was a very fitting spend for a rite of passage young women look forward to. The lyric "coast to coast hear the bell ringing" was clearly inspired by those that get to ring the bell, and the desire to hear it more and more.

I contacted CLIC Sargent and was put in touch with the fundraiser for our area who was a lady called Liz, and we made a plan to have this released on 4th February, World Cancer Day, as a single for the charity. We hit it off immediately, and she became my personal agony aunt. The lyric was sent to the fundraising team for approval, and rightly so, so that they could ensure it wasn't morbid and depressing. Once they had given us the green light, we took it to the studio. There was a lot riding on this and I struggled with the musical side more than usual. Chris had a large input, working a lot on the arrangement and production of it. We got a first draft together and I had an idea. Cancer touches so many of us that I had the idea of opening the studio for a day to invite anyone – sufferers, carers, people who'd lost people, or anyone who wanted to help to come and sing on it, regardless of their musical prowess. We were featured on local TV and had a fantastic day recording backing vocals and gang vocals. The coda section at the end has got 105 tracks of backing vocals on it, which includes a number of our students, choir members and singers from my mum's barbershop chorus Solent Sounds. We were really touched by who turned up to sing, and had a great day.

A wonderful surprise was that Geoff's sister Jayne and her son Eliott turned up to sing. I had not seen Eliott since he was a baby but I did know that he sang in the cathedral choir. I was also not prepared for how much he would remind me of his uncle so it was a bittersweet experience. In the heat of the moment, I asked Eliott to sing a solo for me, which he graciously did. Originally it was just one line, but on a repeated listen we got him back in at a later date to sing a complete half chorus, which rounded it off better for me. It was a beautiful touch to have the spirit of Geoff on there too. When everyone left after the recording session, I promptly burst into tears, with joy, grief, anger, gratitude and exhaustion from all of the above. Creativity is cathartic, for better or for worse.

'Already A Hero' was for Caity and inspired by Caity, but when it came to releasing it, I was also in touch with many other parents and carers via a special online support group administrated by CLIC Sargent. I invited everyone to send photos of their kids – whatever they wanted to send – to be included in a video to promote the song. Inundated with photos, I set about getting them all together, hoping that

I was going to fit them in. As fate would have it, we had exactly the right amount. It makes for a powerful piece of film, featuring children from as young as four months to 18 years old with all kinds of different cancers, including Caity with her beautiful smile and little bald head, bless her, at around round three of chemotherapy.

My artistic intention at this point is to seek light in the darkness. To spend my energy and efforts spreading positivity, finding and focusing on the good. This was a life lesson in this situation, and certainly helped reduce the scars I earned during this chapter in our lives. I have told Caity that I believe, in the long run, she will live a more fulfilling life because of this experience. Just like losing Geoff made me confront my mortality at such a young age, and resolve to live life to the full, Caity has had a similar experience. I'm sure she'll make good of this.

The sales of this song all go to CLIC Sargent – 100% of single revenue and £1 from every CD album sold.

Track 7:
Keep It Simple

Sometimes it's time to write the next story
Give up the grief that got us here
Sometimes it's time to give up the glory
Walk on ahead without so much fear

It's all so complicated, but

Keep it simple, keep it true
Never lose sight of that part of you that can
Sing and smile and dance all the while
Keep it simple

Sometimes it's time to let go of anger
It's all in the past just leave it there
Sometimes it's time to be a bit stronger
Make sure the people you love know you're there

It's all so complicated, but

Keep it simple, keep it true
Never lose sight of that part of you that can
Sing and smile and dance all the while
Keep it simple, keep it true

Keep it true
Keep it true
Keep it true
Keep it simple, keep it true

In contrast to a lot of the big production tunes on this album, this acoustic, singer-songwriter track is much more stripped back and mellow in arrangement. It's a testament to how, in a world fighting to overcomplicate everything, sometimes it's best to keep it simple. As my artistry has developed over the years, there are some sounds that keep coming back. This is one we've come to call the 'Beautiful Monday sound', meaning that this song could have sat quite happily on that album and been in good company. Embracing the natural and simple sound, Pete's organic strings completed this track for me. In the knowledge of the stories that have come earlier in this book, the lyric is pretty self-explanatory. Letting go, being true to yourself, being strong and being there.

Track 8:
No One To Thank Or Blame

Turn your face to the rain, and onward
Steel yourself for the game, and onward
You stand alone, no one to thank
You stand alone, no one to blame

No one to blame
No one to blame

This is the re-recorded version that we perform live in the trio at the time of writing, and will be used for the final scene of the movie that I mentioned earlier. We've made significant changes to the bass line to bring out the angrier side of the dark, and thinned out the harmony instruments, for a more contemporary mix. It's a punchier, less whimsical effect.

Track 9:
First Time

I want you to be my first time
To hold you all night long
This gift will never leave you
To last your whole life long

I want to hear you say, some day that's far away,
Remember the first time?
The magic of the night, two butterflies in flight
Two hearts beating in time.

I want you to be my first time
To hold you all night long
This gift will never leave you
To last your whole life long

Just look into my eyes, this can be no surprise
Tonight we're together
So close the door and stay, there is no other way
We've known it forever, and ever baby.

I want you to be my first time
To hold you all night long
This gift will never leave you
To last your whole life long

Stay, stay with me for the first time, it's the first time.
Lay, lay with me for the first time, it's the first time.

I want you to be my first time.

This was a first for me, being the only song I have ever released under my artist name that was not written by me. This song was written by my friend and fellow muso John Gleadall. He tells the story that this song was born out of his attempt to inspire a group of young songwriters to write a song to raise charitable funds in response to some awful natural disasters. John had prepared a really moving presentation, showing victims of an earthquake in China, floods and other natural disasters. His idea was to inspire the kids to write a song to raise money for the people affected by this.

Alas, they were consumed with another issue. As he says, they were at the age where all their equipment had arrived and all they could think about was getting to use it. Concern over whether or not Phoebe from *Neighbours* was going to sleep with Todd was the topic of discussion. This Australian soap opera was extremely popular in the UK in the 90s, more so than in Australia. John says that the main protagonist who contributed most of the lyrical ideas (that John bashed into an acceptable form!) went on to marry the object of his affections, and their children eventually attended the same school as their parents. A happy ending.

John, Chris and I started performing this song together in about 2017, and have enjoyed recording it together and released it as a fully produced single in the summer of 2018, with 'Say Hello Butterfly' as its B-side (an old tradition I am reluctant to relinquish!), a chalk and cheese release! The album version of 'First Time' features Steve Johnston on trumpets and trombones, and was produced by Chris. Choosing the single artwork was an interesting job – John picked a picture of a beautifully ripe cherry, which would have been hilarious, but I couldn't quite do it! We settled on two teddy bears cuddling, in an attempt to retain some innocence. 'First Time' evolved the more we played it live – we all like to tinker about with each other in a performance situation, and later in 2018 we recorded the acoustic version which is more akin to our live performance of it.

Track 10:
We'll Be Home

We're just about to find it, what we've been looking for
We've been asking all these questions,
and now we know the score

Do do do do, we've reached a milestone
Do do do do let's taste the honeycomb

Coz we're home, oh oh oh
Just take my hand and we'll be home
Coz we're home, oh oh oh
Just take my hand and we'll be home

Now we know we've found it, a place where we belong
Now we've answered all our questions,
and you and me, we're strong

Do do do do, we've reached a milestone
Do do do do let's taste the honeycomb

Coz we're home, oh oh oh
Just take my hand and we'll be home
Coz we're home, oh oh oh
Just take my hand and we'll be home

'We'll Be Home' is a bit of fun, and I really enjoy playing this live. If you've ever been in the audience at one of our shows, you will have experienced the stamping, clapping and shouting lessons before the song starts. I think, really, this is a testament to my settling down at last. For years all I wanted to do was travel, be on the move, roam, get lost, be far away and unfindable. I just wanted to explore and break free of every expectation society had bound me in.

There are elements of that still in my life – I don't think it will ever be gone as long as I live – but I have discovered the joy of being at home, feeling at peace, comfortable and complete. An amazing sense of fulfilment just being with your loved ones on your own sofa.

Track 11:
Say Hello Butterfly

I don't want to waste another dream again,
So push the door and come with me my friend.
There's a great big world of shapes and colours,
A great big sky of stars above us,
And it's right before our eyes.

Say hello butterfly,
It's a new horizon,
Oh oh oh,
Say hello butterfly,
And it's so surprising,
Oh oh oh.
This is your time for reason and rhyme,
Say hello butterfly,
This is your time.

You know butterfly, you deserve to fly.
Butterflies belong in the sky.
Don't be afraid to show your colours,
The sun is coming up above us,
And it's right before our eyes.

Say hello butterfly,
It's a new horizon,
Oh oh oh,
Say hello butterfly,
And it's so surprising,
Oh oh oh.
This is your time for reason and rhyme,
Say hello butterfly,
This is your time.

Now the chrysalis is open,
You can't go back to how it used to be.

Say hello butterfly,
It's a new horizon,
Oh oh oh,
Say hello butterfly,
And it's so surprising,
Oh oh oh.
This is your time for reason and rhyme,
Say hello butterfly,
This is your time.
This is your time.

I really enjoyed making this; it's a simple piano and vocal track about believing in yourself, and having courage. We'd been making a lot of big production pieces when this came together, which is great fun, but I can never last very long before needing to get back to the basic song. A song with a story and production that lets the melody nakedly breathe.

'Say Hello Butterfly' is intended to be an uplifting piece about living life to the full and being true to yourself. As with many of my pieces now, I always hope to reach anyone who needs to hear that message, but it was born out of a series of personal experiences.

On the way to Los Angeles for the premiere of *Stolen Breath*, I was so excited, as I was off for the first time to see a screening of a movie that we'd composed some music for. During the flight I was full of aspirations as I went to meet some people I'd been collaborating with creatively at a distance for quite some time. Instinctively I knew this was a key step to the next level of my artistic fulfilment; I was reflecting on the dreams I'd had when I was younger, and the people I meet who have a dream in this life. It seems to be a different way of existing; to have a dream is to be on a different kind of mission. Just making ends meet is not enough. Fulfilling a dream is like no other feeling I can describe.

It was a morning flight and travelling west, it seems to be the same time of day for hours – one of my loves of travel. It's as if time does stand still for a bit. You pay for it later, of course, but for that moment a certain reflective stillness can be found. Looking down on the clouds will never get old for me. This in particular was such a beautiful flight; the horizon was so clear, I could see the bright icebergs in the ocean, and I was just so excited. I scribbled down some words.

It was a strange time in my life because while all these exciting things were happening, obviously some horrendous things were happening too. Caity was actually still in hospital when I wrote one of the pieces of music for *Stolen Breath*. Previously in my life when things had taken a bad turn, it darkened everything, and I remember those periods of time as holistic misery. This was more of a bittersweet emotional roller coaster. Caity's strength and quiet courage was inspirational, and I just had a feeling she would fly when she could get on the road to recovery. The lyric is fuelled by the feeling that we were both at a positive crossroad in our lives, running our own journeys in parallel, and good things were to follow. These events had changed each of us irreversibly. Now the chrysalis is open, you can't go back to how it used to be...

During my stay in Los Angeles, I had a meeting with a producer following a red carpet event at the beginning of the week. He suggested meeting at a coffee shop on Melrose Avenue, which I think has to be a contender for the longest avenue in the city. I was staying on Melrose in an 'historic' building in Hollywood, and asked at reception if I could walk to the meeting place. Humour ensued and a cab was called for me. I was enormously early, and decided to explore a bit before heading back to the cafe for the meeting later. As I may have mentioned, on the rare occasions I have the time and autonomy, I enjoy an aimless mooch, and just followed my nose along the avenue, with no particular agenda. Before long I came across a store stocking vinyl. Floor to ceiling, like a vintage country house library, it was packed to the gunnels with records. I was in the door like a shot.

Looking around in awe, I noticed a baby grand piano in the back. It's never long when shopping in the States before a sales assistant approaches you, and I got chatting to the proprietor and his jazz enthusiast assistant Jorge. We discussed music, of course, the reason for my trip and the background to his business. Gradually I worked around to asking about the piano; it turned out it belonged to his mother who was a pianist and piano teacher, who encouraged him to achieve the highest accolades as a classical violinist. Enthusiastically they told me that the previous week they had enjoyed a 15-minute jazz and blues concert by Hugh Laurie who now lived in L.A. since becoming the star of the TV show *House*. The proprietor Sandy allowed me to play the piano, but only after Jorge supervised me washing my hands.

Something happened when I sat down at this piano. I felt drawn to it like a magnet. The energy moved through me as I improvised and music flowed out of me. Sandy had a bar stool just to the right of the keyboard and sat over me while I played. I admit that I dislike being scrutinised like that, and much prefer a huge audience a little bit further away.

But I wasn't playing for Sandy, I was playing for me.

And I couldn't stop.

It was a physical feeling.

"Your playing is calm and peaceful," he said to me, which he explained he found refreshing. "Young composers are usually so turbulent and full of anger." I accepted that as a compliment, and didn't correct him by pointing out that I had my angry and turbulent moments. From someone who obviously grew up listening to pianos being played, I was flattered. Three times I tried to get up from this beautiful instrument but I couldn't walk away. It kept calling me back into this ecstatic addictive meditative state. Eventually I knew I was wearing out my welcome and I tore myself away. I bought some records, and as I walked to the front to pay, Sandy presented me with his mother's tiny book *Just Being At The Piano*. A quick glance at the cover showed that it had been categorised by the publisher as 'Music, Buddhism, Zen'. Stunned, I bought several copies, and it remains the book that I wish I'd had when I was a five-year-old piano student. Still, I can always pretend I'm five when I read it. I'm sure in many ways that book came to me at exactly the right time. Perhaps that experience, at least in part, is why I moved over to composing more on piano again.

We made our goodbyes and I was invited to go back there anytime I was in town, and also to use the space for any filming I might like to do, which I still plan on doing at some point. It was almost time for my meeting, and I wandered back to the coffee shop in a state of euphoria.

So what does this have to do with 'Say Hello Butterfly', I hear you ask. Well, when I got home, I was full of songs. Originally, as per old habit, I actually wrote 'Say Hello Butterfly' on guitar and spent a whole evening in the studio recording the guitar part. It was ok, and on the right track for the simple production I had desired for this song, but right at the end of the session I just had a little tinkle on the studio keyboard. Straight away I knew it would have to be piano.

Obvious really, given I was still carrying that book around with me like a comfort blanket. From the off, I wanted only one harmony instrument and minimal production and instrumentation, so I went back to the project the next day and scrapped the guitar part.

All of those experiences are bedded in to 'Say Hello Butterfly'. We released it as the B-side to 'First Time' in the summer, adding Pete's strings onto it for the album version. This song could have comfortably sat on the *Fearless* album and I'm pleased this sound still finds its way into my songs.

Track 12:
Together

Sometimes the sun goes down before I'm really ready
Oo oo oo ooh
Sometimes a cold wind blows and makes me feel unsteady
Oo oo oo ooh
Sometimes I feel alone, it's hard to find a friend but
I know I'll find a smile that's kind

Together we build bridges, hand in hand we're strong
We all have a place, we know where we belong
Together we face winters
Arm in arm we're warm
Raise each voice in harmony
Together

There will be a time you need a helping hand
Oo oo oo ooh
There will be a time you need to swim to land
Oo oo oo ooh
There will be a time you need to take a stand
We know we'll find our strength and pride

Together we build bridges, hand in hand we're strong
We all have a place, we know where we belong
Together we face winters
Arm in arm we're warm
Raise each voice in harmony
Together

When you feel let down it's hard to keep your faith
Put your trust in me and I will keep you safe

Together we build bridges, hand in hand we're strong
We all have a place, we know where we belong
Together we face winters
Arm in arm we're warm
Raise each voice in harmony, you can put your trust in me
Together
We build bridges
We're strong
We all have a place
We belong
Together we build bridges

Raise each voice in harmony
Together

You may recall me telling you about the first weekend Caity was in hospital when we had to tell our choir that Chris might not be able to come to our big event. This song was inspired by that wonderful group of people, and how they gathered around us while Caity was ill. There is something special about singing in a choir, and I had seen other members get very special support and understanding when going through a personal tragedy. It was my first experience of it, previously having always chosen to grieve in private. But I couldn't this time. This affected them too, and I didn't have the strength to put on the brave face I always wore when things were hard. I also couldn't expect Chris to be stoic like me, when he was going through hell on earth.

A tragedy like this really shows you who your friends are. I had experienced that before in situations like relationship breakdown, but it really surprised me this time that support came from the most unlikely places, and not from people you might expect it from. It's a tough lesson to learn, especially when you're already hurting so badly, but I really felt the love of our beautiful little choir. They gave me a purpose and something else to focus on, so I had to keep going. They also forgave me when I did a terrible job of it because I had constant migraines; when I was stoned on prescription beta blockers they laughed with me, and they were always there to lend an ear in the countless hours we felt lost and alone. Regularly, they asked after Caity and how we were doing, but they didn't pry. They worked hard on their music but didn't put undue pressure on us.

One of the few things I miss about having a 'proper job' is having peers. Being a self-employed musician is surprisingly lonely. They gave us a place, a group, a team, and we knew we belonged there. I feel much more shoulder to shoulder with them now, rather than singers and director.

Backstage selfie at the Alexandra Theatre with the Igloo Choir.

Back left to right: Kate Stainton-Ellis, Helen Rose, Andrew Thomas, Viv James. Middle left to right: Harriet Deverill, Helen Godbold, Bob Cheshire, Chris Wood. Front left to right: Hayley Durrant, Carolyn Stallard, DiElle

The song took on a life bigger than that. Whilst I had written it for the choir to sing, the message was so strong, probably because it was so sincere, that I felt moved to record it as a single. It became apparent very quickly that it was leading the pack for a title track. The all-encompassing message summed up everything that was on the album. I asked my good friend and fellow singer-songwriter Eve Williams to duet with me on it, which gave it a Disney-esque, sisterly vibe.

Of course when it came to performing it live, I don't have a sister, but two boys! So we rearranged it between us for the trio, and now these three versions of the song all exist. The choir perform it with armography, beautiful blend and finger lights, Eve and I sing it together when we get the chance, and it is a permanent fixture of our trio show.

Like so many of my songs, this has been inspired by one situation and one group of people, but the message can be seen in all walks of life. It's like my songs teach me to see.

Track 13:
Sunshine After The Waves

Instrumental

I had been reflecting on this connection I have with California, and composed this when I got back from that same trip to Los Angeles, discussing film and TV work.

Our lives are peppered with experiences that we don't realise are shaping us until we have the wisdom of hindsight.

My family did not have a lot of money when I was growing up. My parents were working extremely hard on building their business, something I did not fully understand until I was doing the same thing years later. My mum's youngest sister married an American chap and moved to San Diego when I was small, and it had been a dream of ours as a family to go to the US. My mum and my aunt are very close, and my brother and I really wanted to go to Disneyland and eat massive hamburgers. It was the trip of a lifetime at the time.

The years that I was at secondary school, Mum and Dad's business was really growing at a rate of knots, and the first time we were able to go and see my aunt, I was about 13 years old. It was an amazing trip. Huge Californian beaches as wide and sunny as I had imagined and pizzas the size of dustbin lids. We did all the typical things, Universal Studios, Disneyland, Six Flags Magic Mountain. Despite my mum being afraid of heights, she still went on the Viper, which was the biggest roller coaster in the world at the time complete with seven loop the loops and a corkscrew. We developed a huge love of Mission Beach, which is close to where my aunt still lives. Chris and I went there a few years back and it still holds the magic it did for me as a child, although I have lost my boogie boarding skills somewhat.

I felt alive, excited, yet somehow calm too. I didn't want to come home.

On the last night, we had a BBQ on the beach. As the sun was setting, Dad and I took a stroll up the beach. Being a photographer in a previous life, Dad can't resist a sunset or a sunrise. There was practically no one there, in stark contrast to the hordes of people we had battled with all holiday to get that perfect spot on the beach, not too far from the sea or the ice creams. It was such a peaceful moment. Dad was very ruminative, and was talking to me like he'd deliberately taken me away from the group to give me an important message. I don't know if he had, but it felt that way. It was as if he was sharing with me that he had achieved a dream himself, and that I should have dreams and chase them. The happiest years of my adult life have been while I was doing exactly that. My work taking me back to California in the last few years has been a feeling of coming home, like we were just waiting for that excited little 13-year-old girl to find her way back to that excited calmness.

This piece of music is about that walk with Dad up the beach...

Single: *'Strong'*
Released: 01/08/2018

Strong

Don't listen to the poison of the boys and girls who have given up
Don't give in to the treaty that what's easy is going to be enough
Let your heart say

They're telling you it's over, there's no hope
for the dream that you once had
They're telling you to put up, and shut up,
you're nothing without them
But it's a new day

Keep fighting somehow
The time is always now
I'm gonna show you, show you how to be strong
It's not over when you're still breathing
I'm gonna show you, show you how to be strong

Stop looking for the answer, take a chance
on the things you can't control
Stop worrying that someone is gonna
outrun you to someone else's goal
Make your own way

Keep fighting somehow
The time is always now
I'm gonna show you, show you how to be strong
It's not over when you're still breathing
I'm gonna show you, show you how to be strong

What's your Patronus?

Some of you would have answered that, and some of you would have thought, 'What's a Patronus?'

Are you a Harry Potter fan?

If you're not, this is still a very touching story, and I will explain.

For various reasons, I am, and some of my favourite people are, fans of Harry Potter. The creative in me loves the intricacy of the story, and whilst I'm not generally one to get sucked into hype, I do love a bit of Pottermania. Years ago when I was having a really hard time going through a nasty separation, I decided to read the books from start to finish for a bit of escapism. I thought to myself – by the time I've finished these books, this will all be over. And it was. That was my first reason for having an affection for Harry Potter.

Around the time I was writing this song, at the urging of my step-daughter (who is a huge fan) we went along to the website where you can be sorted into your Hogwarts house, and find out your Patronus (I'm a Hufflepuff and my Patronus is a white stallion). For those of you who are not in the know, the Patronus charm 'expecto Patronum' is the spell that protects you from the soul-destroying beings, 'Dementors', who will suck out your soul. Urban legend has it that the Dementors symbolise depression.

During Caity's cancer treatment her very talented artist cousin Lauren painted her a canvas of her own hand casting her Patronus charm. In art form, in the language that she spoke, she was encouraging Caity not to lose hope, and not to give in to the terror she was feeling at the time. Knowing what this would mean to our daughter, I was so touched. It's an amazing painting, and the thoughtfulness behind it was just beautiful. It's a stunning piece of artwork which took her hours to paint. Even if you're not a Harry Potter fan, I hope you can see the gorgeous gesture between these two lovely young ladies that gave a frightened child hope and courage.

It inspired me and moved me to tears.

This painting was so popular, people started asking for their Patronuses (Patroni? Patronii?) and of course I got mine, as a piece of digital artwork, but I wasn't really sure what to do with it.

Two main things inspired the imagery in this lyric. For a long time, I've lived by the expression "It doesn't matter how many times you fall, it's the number of times you get back up that counts". At the time of writing there's a very funny video on my Facebook page (diellemusicuk) of me talking about this whilst falling off a paddleboard for my 'Beautiful Monday' broadcast. This was my year of weekly live broadcasts of positivity videos at the beginning of the week, which gave rise to my 'Love Mondays' movement. That expression has helped me feel strong at times when I've felt like a failure because everything is going wrong – again. The second is a much more musical influence, although I don't think you'll hear it: the song 'Another Train', written by folk singer Pete Morton, and covered by a band called The Poozies. If you haven't heard it, go and listen to it now. The second verse reflects how I have felt at certain times of tribulation in my life: "When you're standing on your own, your own breath is king". Something else that helps me find strength in difficult times. Perhaps having been let down, trusted the wrong person, or tried something that has failed (I've done that a lot).

Various professional opportunities had developed, and 2018 found us recording with a new producer, Bill Lefler. He's an inspirational musician and his studio Death Star Studios in L.A. is a fantastic creative space. I loved him on sight, as we walked in to find his Christmas tree still up in the middle of May. "Your tree is still up!" I exclaimed, having done exactly the same thing in our studio. "I know, I just like it," he replied, a bit shy. "My Christmas tree is still up! This was just meant to be!" and I was totally over excited for the remainder of the week.

Recording with Billy was an amazing experience and we hope to work with him some more. As a drummer, he was the driving force behind all the percussive clapping and stamping and drumming. The vocal session was also especially enjoyable and Billy handled me really well. Chris, Billy and I all sang gang vocals and shared the stomping and clapping. When I first wrote this song I didn't really like it, not considering it would be something I would sing. Chris urged me to take it to Bill, who made it into something I could never have imagined, and got the vocals out of me that the song needed.

When back from our trip recording with Billy, I was looking for suitable artwork for the new song. Entitled 'Strong' and inspired by the incredible people around me, my Patronus seemed the perfect fit. We had even been gifted tickets to

Harry Potter World at Universal Studios by the recording studio when we were in California. It all seemed to fit.

The image of the white stallion is the spell of my Patronus being cast that Lauren created for me. It's a symbol of strength that epitomises the message this song carries for all people in difficult situations.

Although I sing 'Strong' in the first person, I'm really the recipient of these lessons that I learned through this experience. Other people have taught me how to be strong.

People in the industry call it a 'female empowerment' song. Whilst lyrically it is a celebration of the strong women in my life – my mum, my nan, Caity, my girlfriends – I was happy for the message to be genderless. The fact that the image is a horse feeds into that. The lyric is peppered with my own experiences of shaking off negative messages and voices over the years, and my refusal to give in. Just like all those strong women haven't given in.

EP: *Candlelight*
Released: 01/05/2020

Perhaps I'm evolving; perhaps I'm getting old, but the time has passed for me to just indulge in what I'm feeling. With each year that goes by, I'm learning. Things go wrong every day. Tragedies happen when you're looking the other way. A wise man, Baz Lurhmann, once said "Don't judge yourself too harshly, your failures and successes are half chance, and so are everyone else's" or words to that effect. I may come full circle, as I've been doing this long enough to realise every stage of creativity is just a phase I'm going through, and the time may come again when I do want to indulge in the storm of my emotions. But right now, as I've said, I want to seek for the good. Every awful situation and circumstance I want to learn from like a newborn baby. What can I learn, how can I find positivity, how can I turn something ugly into something beautiful, what constructive lessons can I learn from an awful situation... not to deny the weight of difficulties, but not to be weighed down by them.

There's a Buddhist expression that compassion is like a sole candle in the darkness, from which many other candles can be lit without the first one dimming at all. Even if the others go out, that first candle remains unchanged. I find this something to aspire to, and right now as my artistic endeavour I'm trying to be a candle in the dark. This idea has also inspired a particular song, after which this EP has been named.

Track 1:
Snowdrift

La la la
There's a space between
Where we are and what we've been
Because the snowflake falls
And then the hunger calls
Find the space between
Ooh, ooh, ooh
There's a space between
Where we are and what we've been
Because the snowflake falls
And then the hunger calls
Find the space between

This lyric is both literal and metaphorical. One cold March, we had a snowstorm. Where we live and work is quite remote so when it snows, it's extremely difficult, and sometimes dangerous, getting on and off site. I love a snow day and have a childlike wonder of the magic snowfall brings to the land. As it happens, my dad was flying back from a business trip and Chris offered to drive my mum to the airport in his 4x4 to collect him. All our sessions were cancelled so I was left alone in the studio in a snowdrift.

It was a stressful day for lots of people out there battling the roads, trying to work, get the kids to school, get home from the airport. I knew it was bedlam out there and here I was encapsulated in my own personal snowdrift that was calm, magical and beautiful. It really was as if I'd stepped off the world for the day into my own little snow globe. Absolutely thrilled to be in my own studio; my dream come true.

We had been especially busy during this time, burning the candle at both ends. The metaphorical space the snowstorm gave me was welcome and a lovely breath of fresh air. Although I did feel guilty about enjoying myself when lots of other people were not...

> "There's a space between where we
> are and what we've been."

We've come a long way from those humble dreams so many years ago. From recording songs in my bedroom to having a professional studio, and agents in the USA to send my songs to. Sometimes a 'la la la' and an 'ooh ooh' is all you need to express that excitement and fulfilment. I'd also been in search of space to clear my mind from the multitude of directions it's pulled in every day. Meditation has been extremely effective and encouraging for finding contemplative space in our hectic lives. The time between taking a breath and exhaling, the time between the first light and the full sunrise, passing moments brimming with possibilities.

Track 2:
Look After Me

I looked after you
When you were small
Before you could stand on two feet
You grew and grew
Learned to stand tall
I gave you all you would need
I gave you all of my treasure
You rely on it all beyond measure
I looked after you

Look after me
Look after me
Let me breathe
Swim in a crystal clear sea
Dance with the honeybees
Walk in the trees
Let me breathe
Look after me

They say that pride
Precedes a fall
But it's time to turn down the heat
It's not too late
To give it your all
It's time to vote with your feet
I know you think that you're clever
Even you can't control the weather

Look after me
Let me breathe
Swim in a crystal clear sea
Dance with the honeybees
Walk in the trees
Let me breathe
Look after me

Oh oh let me breathe
Oh oh look after me
Oh oh let me breathe
Oh oh look after me

Look after me
Let me breathe

Let me breathe
Look after me

This is my modern-day protest song of sorts. I always thought I was quite clued up about environmental issues, but I really had no idea how bad pollution has really gotten. I was lucky enough in my early adult life to visit and volunteer at some wonderful conservation projects all over the world, where I learned about the impact of people on the natural world. Placements and education in Ecuador, the Galápagos Islands, Madagascar, the Daintree rainforest, the Great Barrier Reef and Sri Lanka opened my eyes. The Galápagos and Madagascar in particular are places of incredible biodiversity where the impact of the imbalance humankind can bring is so apparent. The magic of snorkelling with penguins and seals or being eye to eye with sifaka lemurs is something I'll never forget. However what I've come to learn is that these places are test tubes and petri dishes for the rest of the world. What is happening there is just condensed and magnified, because of the rarity of their ecosystems. I tried to make changes in my everyday life where I could.

But... I really had no idea about the extent of the problems. Not just here in the UK but all over the world... I feel like it was David Attenborough that brought this discussion to the public consciousness, with the amazing documentaries he's made on conservation issues. Maybe I just missed it, but it seems no one was talking about it with any urgency before that.

It certainly made me realise that what I was doing was not enough, and it's been on my mind more and more.

It's not long before what's on my mind becomes a song. As I've said before, I am the intended recipient of the messages in my songs as much as anybody is – I'm motivating myself to make changes. As well as singing about it, I'm looking at ways in which we can reduce plastic use in our lives, reduce the use of caustic chemicals, use biodegradable kitchen and bathroom products, and have more vegan meals. Conservation of our fragile natural world is always something that I've felt strongly about, but now more so than ever.

As the song starts, you'd be forgiven for thinking that it's about a parent and child, but it's me wondering...

If the natural world had a voice, what might she say? We've let her down. She could be forgiven for being a disappointed parent figure. Everything we needed to evolve to what we are was provided by the natural world. I wondered about the planet's view of the human race, and what we've done to her in such a short amount of time.

But... I still wanted this song to be fun to sing. Balancing my desire for my music to have a positive message with my fear and anger over this topic has been tough. I hope to compensate further for that through my performance, as I don't believe nagging works. I want to inspire people to try a few changes, not make them feel awful. Undeniably, there is anger in this lyric; this really is aimed at the arrogance of those in power who refuse to do enough, or have a hidden agenda.

This lyric is the personification of characteristics of the human race, rather than aimed at ordinary individuals, who, by and large, I believe, are good people. It was my intention to make this a positive message that will educate but not preach, empower but not scaremonger, motivate but not browbeat people, but it has been hard. I've started and abandoned many songs on this topic because I've found it a real challenge to strike the right tone. I'm not sure I've been wholly successful, but since you're here, I can tell you, those were my intentions. Failure, or partial success, is part of the human condition I think.

Education is an amazing thing, and there are so many simple things individuals can do every day to help. But we just don't know about them.

'Look After Me' is a plea. It's going to take all of us to come together over this, and I'm willing that to happen.

Track 3:
Candlelight

Guided by candlelight
Guided by candlelight
Just one tiny spark will light up the dark
By candlelight

Eclipse into nightfall, alone in the dark
Adrift, obscured, cast away
One single candle, the call of the lark
Brings promise of the day

Promise of the day
A candle burning bright
We will find our way
Guided by candlelight
Promise of the day
A candle burning bright
We will find our way
Guided by candlelight

Eclipse into nightfall, alone in the dark
Adrift, obscured, cast away
One single candle, the call of the lark
Brings promise of the day

Guided by candlelight
Guided by candlelight
Just one tiny spark will light up the dark
By candlelight

This song is inspired specifically by the words of the Buddha I mentioned earlier. Those words are

"Thousands of candles can be lighted from a single candle, and the life of the single candle will not be shortened. Happiness never decreases by being shared."
– The Buddha

I also heard Billy Connolly, arguably a very different character, say something very similar in a Comic Relief appeal years ago. Compassion does not expire because you've shown some to somebody. It's not like money that runs out. You can continue to be more and more compassionate without your cup running empty. Just like the spark, it can be a tiny gesture. I think sometimes when someone is in a particularly dark place in their life, a small act of kindness can be like a spark in the darkness. I know it's been like that for me at times.

Compassion is the candle in this story. I can't help but feel that 'finding our way' is a metaphor for overcoming division between people. At the time of writing, there is disconnect and disequilibrium in the air. People feel disenfranchised. People are angry.

Just like the candle, your light will not extinguish because you've lit someone else's candle.

It's an idea I have been inspired by since hearing it when I was young, but it really helped me during some difficult years as an adult.

This song is inspired by this image. Of all the times I've been lost in the dark and needed that one little tiny light to light the way. Of all the times I have been that light, gladly, willingly and with love, and all the times I thought twice about it because of all the times I have been hurt and let down. There have been times in my life when I've not wanted to offer any more of myself, because it has not been reciprocated in the past, or worse, it was forsaken. But so often I was hesitant to offer my light because of a hangover from a previous situation when I'd been let down, and on reflection that was irrelevant to the current circumstance. Unrequited light. I think there's a lyric in there.

Furthermore, I see this in other people. Because someone let me down, or I was disappointed by someone else, I am not going to extend that same courtesy to you now, today. Someone abused my trust years ago, so I will not trust you. I never wanted to live like that, but I feared that my darker years had made a cynic of me. I was looking for a way to refuel my faith in humankind without feeling like I was being taken advantage of. This saying provides me with the perspective I need for that. People can let me down time and time again, but becoming cynical and mistrusting only adds up to a failure in human compassion.

Don't let your light go out, just because other people have not seen its beauty. You have to see it and protect it for yourself.

Closing Words

So, dear reader, I hope you have enjoyed this journey through the murky land of creativity with me. I hope these stories have heightened your enjoyment of music and answered that often-asked question "So what's that about then?" Whilst artistic licence has been applied in the songs, the stories are all as I remember them, and everything I've told you about the songs, to my knowledge, is true. Aside from the fact that Naomi won competitions for her sunflowers. Apparently I imagined that, but she likes this idea, so I plan to give them an award myself. So perhaps by the time you read this, it will be true after all.

I don't know when or if we will cross paths again, but I do always hope to see you in the flesh at an arts centre show, a house concert, or in the virtual world. How or wherever it may be, do say hello and let me know it's you. I'd love to hear from you. Don't be a stranger.

Love from DiElle

www.diellemusic.com

Photo credits

page 48: DiElle

page 102: Glen Jevon

page 112: Beth Whitley

page 140: DiElle

page 167: Glen Jevon

Album design credits

page 11: Photographer Greg Dorling, designer DiElle

page 15: Photographer Greg Dorling, designer DiElle

page 51: Photographer Beth Whitley, album artist Kate Simms, designer DiElle

page 93: Lauren Norton

page 145: Lauren Norton

page 151: Lauren Norton

About the Author

Born in leafy Hampshire, DiElle came from a musical family, one of her earliest memories being of lying under the piano at her nan's house during a family sing song at the age of perhaps four years old. With her mother and father both being musical, there was always music in the house, and DiElle's dad put a guitar in her hand first of all when she was about three. He always played and encouraged his children to play, sing and be creative. Although DiElle had piano lessons at school from the age of five, it was singing that really spoke to her first. Having given her first solo performance at the age of eight, DiElle also channelled her fertile imagination into writing short stories and poetry around this time. This continued until her early teens when her love of guitar flourished and those two creative powers met in the form of songwriting.

Ever curious, DiElle studied voice, music, songwriting and the music business from the age of 11 onwards.

The intervening years were turbulent. Having lost a childhood friend and volunteered in Sri Lanka for a year by her late teens, travel, love and loss fuelled her inspiration, which resulted in producing three studio albums, *Beautiful Monday* in 2009, *Fearless* in 2014 and *Together* in 2017. Infused with a love of original songwriters like Bob Dylan, Joni Mitchell and Carole King from her parents' record collection, DiElle is a lover of a good story, a singable melody and a lyric inspired by life experience. With an eclectic taste in music, and a deep belief in it being a healer and a means of communication for people from all walks of life, her creations have covered folk, rock, pop, reggae and cinematic styles as well as a more traditional acoustic 'singer-songwriter' genre. DiElle's music career has spanned the greatest changes in the music industry, which is now unrecognisable from where she began. A love of creating, singing, storytelling and sharing music perseveres for her.

DiElle now lives back in Wickham, her childhood stamping ground, with her own studio where she works composing and teaching music, as well as producing her own live shows. With her fourth studio album release, the EP *Candlelight*, she wanted to do something different, to revive the excitement of having something in your hand when you get new music, something she remembers well from childhood that is now lost in the current trend of digital downloads and streaming. Having played with many musicians, DiElle is currently performing in an acoustic trio with formidable musicians John Gleadall and Chris Wood, and having the time of her life to boot.